SPIRITUAL DIMENSIONS
OF THE
HOLY CANONS

Lewis J. Patsavos

Spiritual Dimensions
of the
Holy Canons

HOLY CROSS ORTHODOX PRESS
Brookline, Massachusetts

© Copyright 2003 Holy Cross Orthodox Press
Published by Holy Cross Orthodox Press
50 Goddard Avenue
Brookline, Massachusetts 02445

LIBRARY OF CONGRESS CATALOGING–IN–PUBLICATION DATA

Patsavos, Elias I.
  Spiritual dimensions of the holy canons / Lewis J. Patsavos.
    p. cm.
Includes bibliographical references.
  ISBN 1-885652-68-2 (pbk. : alk. paper)
  1. Canon law, Orthodox Eastern—Sources. I. Title.
LAW
262.9′819—dc22

                              2003014326

To His Eminence Archbishop Iakovos
Spiritual Father – Pastor – Mentor

Whose inspiring example has guided me a lifetime.

CONTENTS

PART ONE

INTRODUCTION TO ORTHODOX
CANONICAL TRADITION

PRESUPPOSITIONS OF
CANONICAL TRADITION

Pastoral Issues of Canonical Tradition

PART TWO

APPENDIX

CLASSIFICATON OF

CANONICAL TRADITION

I. CANONS RELATED TO ADMINISTRATION

II. Canons Related to Penitential Discipline Invoked in Ecclesiastical Courts

III. Canons Related to Penitential Discipline Invoked by Spiritual Fathers during Holy Confession

IV. CANONS RELATED
TO ECCLESIASTICAL COURT PROCEDURE

V. CANONS RELATED TO MONASTICISM

FOREWORD

The canonical tradition of the Orthodox Church embodies a most precious dimension of ecclesiastical life. The parameters of this dimension are defined by the fine intersection of theology and jurisprudence, sophisticated disciplines which not only serve to promote the good order of the Church, but which keep all Her members aligned in a proper relationship with the living God. In our quest toward the Kingdom of Heaven, a journey which we human beings undertake with all our frailties and weaknesses, the Holy Canons serve as tried and trusted signposts, pointing the way toward salvation in Christ, our Immortal King and God.

This quest for eternal salvation lies at the very heart of the Orthodox canonical tradition. It is this quest that has indelibly molded the outward form and structure of the Holy Canons over the course of the life of the Church. Seen through this lens, there is a clear spiritual dimension to the Holy Canons, a dimension that essentially defines the Orthodox Christian understanding of jurisprudence, rendering it whole, complete, and sanctified.

From a pastoral perspective, the spiritual dimensions of the Holy Canons challenge our abilities to examine situations with precision, and to respond to these situations accordingly, always balancing judgment with mercy. Simultaneously, the spiritual dimensions of the Holy Canons challenge our capacities to tolerate the ambiguities that arise from aspects of the eastern ecclesial canonical tradition which are entirely unique in character and which are noticeably absent from secular juridical models, such as the principle of *economia*.

However, the spiritual dimensions of the Holy Canons may not always be easily discernible, thus requiring a special effort on the part of the theologian in order to show the tremendous spiritual value of the Canons. This enterprise, a labor of love and expertise, is carried out through such examinations and studies as the present, very valuable and concise compendium offered by Dr. Lewis Patsavos. This book, *Spiritual Dimensions of the Holy Canons*, has as its chief aim, to elucidate the fundamentals of the Canonical Tradition of the Orthodox Church—to raise the *spirit* of the law to the surface of our ecclesial consciousness and, by so doing, to communicate the essence of a law which is written *not on tablets of stone but on tablets of human hearts*. (2 Corinthians 3:3).

To clergy, concerned laity, and in particular students of theology, this compendium carries also a useful practical application, communicating the reality that the Holy Canons are not legalistic remnants of an age long past; quite the contrary, they are vivid reminders of Christ's authority as exercised within His Church throughout the centuries—living testimonials that it is Christ Himself *who has made us competent to be ministers of a new covenant* (2 Corinthians 3:6). This is the awesome pastoral legacy that we uphold in applying the spiritual insights of the Holy Canons to pastoral situations, insights which remain as valid as ever for contemporary persons living in a contemporary age.

On behalf of the Greek Orthodox Archdiocese of America, I wish to thank Dr. Patsavos for his vital contribution to this important field, which keenly penetrates the letter of the law, unearthing the vast spiritual riches that reside at its core. It is my fervent prayer that God may grant every opportunity for growth to all who read this work, that they may be led unfailingly to the beauty and immensity of the Spirit of God, Whose law is love, freedom, truth, and the ceaseless imitation of Him.

† DEMETRIOS
Archbishop of America

PREFACE

The purpose of this publication is twofold: to provide the reader with a concise overview of Orthodox canonical tradition and an outline of the subject matter addressed by the holy canons. It is, therefore, made up of two parts, a survey of Orthodox Canon Law and a listing of the holy canons by subject.

At the same time, my intent is to stress the spiritual dimension of Orthodox canonical tradition. My hope is that the reader will be guided to understand and appreciate that Orthodox Canon Law is not another human system of law. Rather, it is a living tradition which incorporates elements of both theology and jurisprudence. Of these elements, the former predominate, thereby giving it its unique character. The uniqueness of Orthodox canonical tradition lies in the fact that it is spiritual in its approach.

By making the present volume available in its current format, it is my hope that both the theological and spiritual dimensions of Orthodox canonical tradition become thoroughly apparent. Although constituting a unit, this work was originally published as three separate articles. The first, "The Canonical Tradition of the Orthodox Church," appeared in *A Companion to the Greek Orthodox Church*, ed. by F.K. Litsas, New York: Greek Orthodox Archdiocese, 1984, 137-47; the second, "Lived Experience and Theoretical Differences in the Approach to Law and Discipline in the Eastern and Western Churches," in the volume *Rightly Teaching the Word of Your Truth*, ed. by N.M. Vaporis, Brookline, MA: Holy Cross Orthodox Press, 1995, 185-202; and the third, "The Interface of Pastoral Ministry and the Holy Canons," in *Kanon* 15 (1999), 179-95. Appreciation is hereby expressed to each of the publishers for permission granted to reproduce these articles together as one volume with appropriate revisions where necessary.

A word of special thanks is due to my respected colleagues, Rev. Dr. Alkiviadis C. Calivas, for his encouragement in preparing this work, and Rev. Dr. Theodore Stylianopoulos, for his insightful suggestions in improving the text. My gratitude is expressed as well to Mr. John Metakis and Mr. Herald Gjura of Holy Cross Orthodox Press, for their invaluable assistance and cooperation throughout the preparation of the manuscript. I am deeply in their debt.

Lewis J. Patsavos
July 20, 2003
Feastday of the Prophet Elijah

CHAPTER ONE

INTRODUCTION TO ORTHODOX CANONICAL TRADITION[*]

The Theological Basis of the Church's Law[1]

Canon Law. Although generally referred to as canon law, such a name given to the Church's law suggests a parallel to secular law. It would be more correct to call it the tradition of the holy canons, since they are the object of its concern. This law of the Church, her canonical tradition, is an outgrowth of the holy canons; and it appears on the surface to have much in common with secular law, involving persons invested with authority (bishops), as well as the means of creating, formulating, interpreting, executing, validating, amending, and revoking laws (through synods or conciliar actions).

Church and Secular Law. The apparent similarity of the Church's law to secular law led some to contest the integrity of the former. Yet without it, it is clear, there would be many varied problems besetting the Church. In the last analysis, the Church's law exists to safeguard particular interests from the arbitrary intervention of superior interests. It should not be understood as subjecting a person to subservience, but as guaranteeing his freedom. Contrary to what some have believed, the Church's law differs essentially from secular law. Its difference lies mainly in the premise that the original source of canon law is

1

found in the will of God to establish his Church on earth. Consequently, the source of its authority stems from the will of God. Furthermore, the Church's law differs from secular law in purpose (humanity's salvation), time (extending beyond this life into the next life), scope (including one's conscience), and place (the universal Church).

The Main Goal of Canon Law. When our Lord entrusted the work of salvation to the Church, which is a society of mortal men and women, he obliged her to provide herself with the necessary means of survival. This was to assist her in organizing herself, in overseeing the orthodoxy of her members, and in guarding against factions. In short, he obliged her to provide herself with a set of rules to live by. In so doing, the Church as a community of faith came to be associated with a juridical organization. This does not mean, however, that the community of faith was thereby reduced to a legal institution. The distinction is an important one.

Historical Background. Our Lord himself instituted some elements of such an order. He preached the gospel of salvation to his contemporaries but did not leave to their arbitrary will the task of spreading his message for the benefit of future generations. He assigned that task to a group of men chosen with divine care and wisdom, the apostles, who were clearly aware of the sacred mission with which they were entrusted by the Master. Following his ascension, he endowed them with the authority to make the decisions necessary to assure the continuation of the work he had already begun. Decisions such as the election of Matthias to take the place of Judas among the apostles and setting the conditions for entry into the Church were made at the outset. In fact, they constitute the beginnings of the Church's law, in the development of which Saint Paul played a predominant role.

With the spread of the Christian community throughout the entire area of the Mediterranean, the initial organization of the Church soon had to be extended. During this stage of growth, a hierarchy was developed and new conditions of life modeled after the teachings of Christ came into existence. It thus became necessary to define the status of the believer within the Christian community and society at large.

This organization was only rudimentary, but it clearly was a definite framework. It is quite evident that the Church in her primitive period had no precisely defined juridical organization, much less a technique or science of law. However, all the elements of a true juridical organization were there. Those persons invested with authority made rules and demanded strict adherence to them. Synods came out unsparingly against those who threatened the unity of the Church and the purity of her doctrine. They did not hesitate, furthermore, to impose severe sanctions upon those who opposed her discipline. It was the First Ecumenical Synod of Nicaea (325) which referred to canons as the disciplinary measures of the Church. The distinction, therefore, between "kanones," the disciplinary measures and rules adopted by the Church, and "nomoi," the legislative actions taken by the state, came about quite early.

Canon Law in the Christian Society. The law which emerged from these earliest times was developed in response to the needs of the ecclesiastical community. During both good and bad periods of the Church's history, her law has adapted itself constantly to the circumstances of the time, up to the present day. The collections of laws which the Church has promulgated in no way detract from her exalted status and sacred character. They reflect a certain imperfection; however, this imperfection lies not in the institution of the Church but in those individuals of whom it is composed. As an institution of divine origin composed of human beings, the Church is at the same time both a human and a divine institution. It might be said that it is at the crossroads of the finite and the infinite, the created and the uncreated, the human and the divine.

Our Lord entrusted the work of salvation to his Church – that is, to human beings. Because of this, he gave the Church roots in history and subjected her to temporal contingencies. It is in the Church and through the Church that human beings must in principle attain their salvation. When we speak of the Church, we speak of a society. As such, she is governed by rules which determine her organization and her relations to her members and to those outside her fold.

Finally, it must not be forgotten that the Church is not to be identified with her rules. The Church indeed has rules, but she has much else besides. She has within her treasures of another order and another value besides her canons. She has her theology, her spirituality, her mysticism, her liturgy, her morality. And it is most important not to confuse the Gospel and the Pedalion (collection of canons), theology and legislation, morality and jurisprudence. Each is on a different level and to merge them completely would be to fall into a kind of heresy. The canons are at the service of the Church; their function is to guide her members on the way to salvation and to make following that way easier.

The Church's legislation is only one aspect of her life, and above all does not represent her essence. The Church is the mystical body of Christ; however, her presence in history necessarily has brought forth a juridical system and juridical institutions. Law indeed has its purpose in the Church and is justifiable. But it must also be recognized that this law is of a special character. The uniqueness of canon law, which sets it apart from secular law, is due to the special character of the Church it serves. Because it shares to some extent in the exalted mission of the Church, it differs from all other systems of law.

The Composition of the Church's Law

The Essence of Canon Law. Given the above justification for the existence of the Church's law, it now remains to define what in fact it is and of what it is composed. The Church's law, commonly referred to as canon law, is the system of law emanating from the holy canons, which derive from the Church on her own authority. The Church, as has already been stated, is at the same time both a human and a divine institution. As an institution with a human element, the Church has need of laws to govern her organization, her relations to her members, to those outside her fold, to the state, and to other religious and secular bodies. Nevertheless, the Church's law is first and foremost spiritual, since its main purpose is the spiritual growth of the faithful. Furthermore, its main object of concern is the inner disposition and intention behind one's actions.

Collections of Canon Law. The holy canons, which are the basis of the Church's canonical tradition, stem from three main sources: ecumenical synods (representing the universal Church), local synods (subsequently ratified by the ecumenical synods as representing the tradition of the universal Church), and the fathers of the Church. All of these canons, which number about one thousand, are contained in several collections. The one most widely used today in the Greek-speaking Orthodox Churches is the Pedalion (the "Rudder"), which takes its name from the metaphor of the Church depicted as a ship. As the ship which is guided safely to its destination by means of a rudder, in like manner are the members of the Church guided on their voyage through life by means of the holy canons.

Unlike the canon law of the Roman Catholic Church, the canon law of the Orthodox Church has not been codified. Neither is it prescriptive in character, anticipating a situation before it actually takes place; instead, it is corrective in nature, responding to a situation once it has occurred. Because of the absence of a universal codification binding upon all autocephalous or self-governing Orthodox churches, great importance is attached to the local legislation of each of these churches. Canon 39 of the Sixth Ecumenical Synod (also known by the names Penthekti, Quinisext or Synod "in Trullo") held in 691, recognized the right of a local church to have its own special laws or regulations: "For our God-bearing fathers also declared that the customs of each church should be preserved...." Such laws or regulations, however, must always reflect the spirit of the Church's universal law as found in the holy canons.

The Canonical Tradition. The overriding consideration in the acceptance of a local church's custom as law is the spiritual well-being of the members of Christ's mystical body. What is of importance is how people in any age or place may best serve and worship God. It is obvious that what is well intentioned for the Church as a whole may not be so well suited to some particular local conditions. Similarly, what is good for one age or place may under different conditions constitute a hindrance. Thus it is that the Church's canonical tradition has such regard for local custom. Having evolved within the context of local conditions, it best expresses the mind of the local church on how the cause of God may be served in her special conditions. Custom is the continuously expressed will of God's people. The significance of this statement becomes apparent when one realizes that the last ecumenical synod with universally binding legislation occurred twelve centuries ago (787 A.D.). Consequently, the emergence and growth of local custom especially since that time is what in large measure has sustained the Orthodox Church throughout the ages.

The growth and development of a local custom that acquires the force of law is what gives to the Church's canonical tradition its great flexibility. Local laws or regulations are the means by which the Church's universal canonical tradition adapts itself to changing circumstances. Although this is true, it must not be supposed that any local custom automatically establishes itself as part of the Church's canonical tradition. For that, certain conditions must be met. In the first place, it must be the conviction of the ecclesiastical community concerning a certain act repeated in the same way for a long time. Therefore, two main conditions are necessary for the acceptance of custom as law: it must have enjoyed a long and steady practice, and the consensus of opinion must be that it has the force of law. In order for custom to be accepted as a source of the Church's canonical tradition, it must be in full harmony with holy tradition and scripture, as well as doctrine.

One example of local legislation is the Charter of the Greek Orthodox Archdiocese of America. According to article 1 of the charter, the Archdiocese is "an Eparchy of the most Holy Apostolic and Patriarchal Ecumenical Throne of Constantinople... governed by the Holy Scriptures, the Sacred Tradition, the Holy Canons, this Charter, the Regulations promulgated by it pursuant hereto, and as to canonical and ecclesiastical matters not provided-for herein, by the decisions of the Holy and Sacred Synod of the Ecumenical Patriarchate". As a province of the Ecumenical Patriarchate, the first-ranking see among the autocephalous Orthodox Churches, the American Archdiocese is an ecclesiastical body deriving its authority from a central source. The various components comprising its canonical structure are elements included in the legal system of every local Orthodox Church.

Codification of Canon Law. Because of the apparent dissimilarity among the legal systems of the various autocephalous churches, there are those who consider a uniform codification of the Church's law a near impossibility, and that a separate codification for each of them will be necessary. Then there are those who reject codification outright as conflicting with the spiritual essence of Orthodoxy. They believe that the deep unity which exists among all the Orthodox Churches in faith and sacramental life can continue to be maintained according to the local traditions of each autocephalous church.

Nevertheless, both views mentioned above have been challenged by the former Metropolitan Bartholomaios of Philadelphia (now Ecumenical Patriarch) in his article entitled "A Common Code for the Orthodox Churches".[2] He reminds those who stress the dissimilarity among the legal systems of the autocephalous churches that within Orthodoxy there is basically a single law, whose most important sources are common to all the Orthodox Churches. Furthermore, "the Orthodox Church is neither the sum of a number of independent Churches, nor a federation of Churches with an external, inter-church law, but one Church, the Body of Christ, within which the local Churches are expressions of the one, undivided, living, holy, catholic Church in various places".[3] On the other hand, those who reject codification on the grounds that it conflicts with the essence of Orthodoxy are reminded that the Church is not only a charismatic body; she is an institution with both a divine and a human element; and, as such, she is in need of a code of laws to enhance the evolution of ecclesiastical life and to assure the further development of Orthodox canon law.

The Characteristics of the Church's Law

Applicability of Canon Law. Any discussion of the characteristics of the Church's law must necessarily address the question of the applicability of the holy canons to today's realities. Viewpoints expressed on this vital issue range from one extreme to the other, and are mutually exclusive. On the one hand, there are those who revere the letter of the canons. But as has already been remarked, "no one seems to absolutize all of them".[4] Then there are those who deny the relevancy of the entire body of canons in its present state. Obviously, both views leave little room for a conciliatory approach but rather tend to polarize.

In order to effect a rapprochement between the widely divergent views just mentioned, the question must first be asked: How were the holy canons meant to be understood? Nicholas Afanasiev, in his article entitled "The Canons of the Church: Changeable or Unchangeable?"[5] offers a formula which might be acceptable to all factions: "Canons are a kind of canonical interpretation of the dogmas for a particular moment of the Church's historical existence. . . They express the truth about the order of Church life, but rather than expressing this truth in absolute forms, they conform to historical existence".[6] Such a formula recognizes the absolute validity of all the canons as practical aids which gave expression to doctrinal truths at some point in history. Some of these aids, however, it sees as having outlived the purpose for which they were originally intended, i.e., they are conditioned by time. Consequently, they cannot give expression to doctrine without causing distortion, simply because they were intended for another era. This, of course, cannot be said of all the canons, since there are many which express doctrine as clearly today as when they were first adopted by the Church. Therefore, while some canons continue to reflect doctrine in practice, others do not and must be seen in historical context in order to be understood. The following example will illustrate this point.

It is a doctrine of the Church that the ecclesiastical hierarchy is an institution ordained by God. There are canons which express this doctrine, but in conformity with the era in which they were adopted. Canon 5 of the Holy Apostles forbids a bishop, presbyter, or deacon to put away his wife under the pretext of religion. A later decision of the Sixth Ecumenical Synod introduced celibacy for the episcopate and directed that all previously ordained bishops should leave their wives. This synod was correct when it said that it was publishing the new decree "not with any intention of setting aside or overthrowing any legislation laid down of people and for their advancement."[7] The apostolic canon expressed a doctrine concerning the ecclesiastical hierarchy, but in conformity with its era. When the historical conditions of life changed, so too did the manner in which this doctrine was expressed.

Pastoral Significance of Canon Law. The canons ought also to be understood as pastoral guidelines. As such, they should serve as models upon which subsequent ecclesiastical legislation is based whenever possible. The canons of the fathers, in particular, reflect the pastoral nature of their content. The fathers who wrote them did not think that they were writing legislative texts. In most cases, they were either responding to the questions put to them by individuals seeking their counsel, or else expressing their views on matters of grave concern to the Church. Because of their pastoral sensitivity and the high esteem in which they were held, these fathers greatly influenced both their contemporaries and succeeding generations. As a result, the directives contained in the canons of the fathers prior to the Sixth Ecumenical Synod were recognized by the second canon of that synod as equal in authority to the synodal canons themselves. In fact, several of the canons of St. Basil specifically were included among the canons of the Sixth Ecumenical Synod.

The fathers whose canons appear in our canonical collections exerted no less influence upon the development and formation of the canons of other synods. Consequently, the pastoral nature evident in the canons of the fathers is also easily discernible in the canons of the synods. It is because of this characteristic that the canons have been referred to as "fruits of the Spirit," whose purpose is to assist humankind in its quest for salvation. Certainly such a lofty purpose can only be appreciated when the canons are understood as pastoral guidelines and not as legislative texts. Viewed simply as legislative texts, the canons differ little from laws to be upheld rigidly and absolutely. Recognized, however, as the pastoral guidelines which in fact they are, the canons serve the purpose for which they were intended with compassion and flexibility. It is this latter understanding of the canons which makes comprehensible the exercise of "economy" as practiced in the Orthodox Church today.

The Concept of "Economy." Unlike secular law or Mosaic law, the purpose of the Church's law is the spiritual perfection of her members. Mere application of the letter of the law is replaced by a sense for the spirit of the law, and adherence to its principles. This purpose is the determining factor when authority is granted to apply the law when circumstances warrant according to each individual case. The spirit of love, understood as commitment to the spiritual perfection of the individual, must always prevail in the application of the law. The abolition of the letter of the law by the spirit of the law has led to the institution of "economy," exercised in non-essential matters. Through "economy," which is always an exception to the general rule, the legal consequences following the violation of a law are lifted.

"Economy" is granted by the competent ecclesiastical authority and has not so much the character of urgency as it does the character of compassion for human frailty. The character of compassion is justified by the Church's ardent desire to prevent any adverse effects from the strict observance of the law in exceptional circumstances. The premise upon which an exception is granted is the general welfare of all concerned. This premise exists in all systems of law but it finds its fullest expression in the Church's law. As the law of grace, it is characterized primarily by the spiritual attributes of compassion, pastoral sensitivity, and forgiveness.

"Economy" is not something to be applied at random or arbitrarily. It is governed by defined guidelines which must be strictly adhered to by the competent ecclesiastical authority granting it. First and foremost, exception from a law which has been endowed with universal recognition and validity is not possible. It is only from a law that has not been endowed with such authority that a person can be released, if this is deemed spiritually beneficial.

The right to exercise "economy" is the sole prerogative of the legislator (council or holy synod of bishops). This right can in turn be delegated to individual bishops by the corporate authority of the synod. This delegation must, however, be within the limits prescribed by the canons and according to the express authorization of one's superior legislative authority. This is the spirit of canon 2 of Ancyra: "It is likewise decreed that deacons who have sacrificed [to pagan idols] and afterwards resumed the conflict shall enjoy their other honors, but shall abstain from every sacred ministry, neither bringing forth the bread and the cup, nor making proclamations. Nevertheless, if any of the bishops shall observe in them distress of mind and meek humiliation, it shall be lawful to the bishops to grant more indulgence, or to take away [what has been granted]".[8]

As evidenced by the phrase: "it shall be lawful to the bishops to grant more indulgence, or to take away [what has been granted]" in canon 2 of Ancyra, "economy" may be both a more lenient or a more strict observance of the rule. Consequently, "economy" is any deviation from the norm. The exercise of "economy" ceases if its cause no longer exists or the basis for its application rested upon false or pretended grounds. Once "economy" has been applied, the normative practice is restored as before. Furthermore, temporary departure from the normative practice through "economy" does not set a precedent.

The institution of "economy" has been actively invoked throughout the history of the Orthodox Church. This is perhaps due in part to liberal trends of thought in the cultural milieu within which the Orthodox Church flourished. Although authority in the exercise of "economy," especially in matters of great importance, rests with the synod of bishops of each local church, this authority, as indicated, can be delegated to individual bishops as well. The ecumenical synod, as supreme administrative, legislative and judicial body in the Church, holds the ultimate authority in the exercise of "economy". It alone can alter or overrule the decision of any subordinate ecclesiastical authority. In the realm of conscience, however, it is the spiritual father who has been entrusted with the authority to exercise "economy" according to his good judgment. The determining factor in its application, however, must always be the spiritual welfare of the penitent.

Canonical Discipline. Since the realm of conscience has been mentioned, a final word remains regarding the character of canonical discipline. Following a penitent's admission of guilt in the sacrament of penance, the spiritual father determines whether acts of penance ("epitimia") should be prescribed. These acts of penance may include fasting, prostrations, prayer, acts of charity, or minor excommunication (temporary exclusion from holy communion) among others. Acts of penance must not be confused with punishment in the sense of retribution for evil committed. They must not have any element of vindictive punishment about them. On the contrary, the purpose of the Church's canonical discipline is both pastoral and pedagogical. It seeks both to correct and reform the repentant sinner and to protect the community from the resulting sin. Consequently, by depriving the sinner of holy communion for a time, it seeks to impress upon the individual the gravity of his sin. At the same time, if the sin is publicly known, it seeks to demonstrate that certain acts are, beyond any doubt, inadmissible for everyone.

The Church, which is the mystical body of Christ, utilizes her own means to achieve the salvation of all her members. Although the Church is simultaneously a human and a divine institution, her earthly aspect is predominantly spiritual. So long as the Church retains this aspect of her existence, the holy canons together with the canonical tradition emanating from them will be an essential part of her earthly life. It is the Church's canons and canonical tradition which assure the external means of security within which the life of the spirit is nurtured and preserved.

CHAPTER TWO

PRESUPPOSITIONS OF CANONICAL TRADITION [9]

The Church as Divine-Human Communion[10]

Orthodox pastoral ministry is ecclesiological and cannot be understood apart from the mystery of the Church. The Church as a divine-human communion in Christ is the only place in which pastoral work can be fruitful. She is the beginning and end of pastoral ministry because pastoral ministry presupposes the Church. Furthermore, its goal is the assimilation of the believer into the Church, the body of Christ, as effectively and conscientiously as possible, so that the process which leads to spiritual perfection (theosis) will result.

The holy canons stress the nature of the Church as communion between God and human beings in Christ. This communion is effected through the divine mysteries, particularly the holy eucharist, as well as through the other gatherings of the church body.

Unity in the Church, characterized as catholic (all encompassing) unity, is granted by God as a gift. This, in fact, is what distinguishes it from the unity of human beings. In the catholic unity of the Church, the believer becomes a "whole" ("catholic") person ("katholikos anthropos"), i.e., one who lives the fullness of the life in Christ.

Such a believer, whose "catholic" image is the goal of Orthodox pastoral ministry, is one who overcomes every partiality and fragmentation. Such a person is totally open to God and to God's children, his fellow human beings. He lives the fullness of God's truth and the fullness of God's love. His frail, fallen, ego-centric individualism is restored to wholeness and transformed into theocentric communion. The person who is "catholic" (i.e., Orthodox) in belief and "catholic" (i.e., virtuous) in behavior, lives the Church's truth in a harmonious and balanced way and follows the evangelical virtues without absolutizing elements of the faith, which would lead to heresy or pietism. He does not separate doctrine from ethics, and neither does he discard a christocentric ethic for pietism.

Also, he does not confine himself to factions, considering them as the authentic means of salvation and of renewal in the Church. He does not absolutize human trends of the times, and neither does he reject as anachronistic the fruits of the Holy Spirit, i.e., the life-giving tradition and canonical decrees of the Church.

The "catholic" believer has overcome the antithesis between conservatism and progressivism. He is conservative because he seeks to preserve the eternal truth of the Church, and at the same time progressive because he seeks to advance her truth day by day. The saints and fathers of the Church are the models of the "catholic" believer and for this very reason the guides of both shepherds and flock in their journey towards catholicity.

The genuineness of the Church's pastoral ministry lies in whether it directs the faithful towards catholicity (truth/virtue). Therefore, true pastors of the Church do not preoccupy themselves with changing and updating the Church's decrees for the sake of change. Rather, they are concerned more with changing and transforming themselves and the members of their flock into "catholic" believers through their participation in the catholic truth and life of the Church. Such an approach alone transforms without being transformed, changes without being changed, and saves one in Christ without being saved by its alliance with the world.[11]

Because it is the whole life and truth of the Church which makes one a "catholic" believer, Orthodox pastoral ministry directs the faithful to a catholic participation in the Church and in whatever constitutes and reveals the Church. This includes her divine worship, her spoken word, her mysteries, her saints, her canonical tradition, and whatever expresses the Church as the body of the living Christ, and as the visible and invisible communion of the Holy Spirit.

The Church's Revelation of Truth[12]

The goal of pastoral ministry is to familiarize the Christian flock with the truth preserved in the Church's holy tradition. This truth is not a rational concept but a hypostatic reality, the divine and human Christ, the Church's head and her body. Therefore, pastoral ministry as the revelation of this truth is essentially different from the purely humanistic approach of responding to the worldly needs of human beings.

Because of the strong influence of anthropocentrism and secularism, contemporary pastoral ministry is in danger of limiting its task to purely humanistic activity and of forgetting that its principle mission is the "transmission of truth". In order for it to rescue the true mission entrusted to it by our Lord, pastoral ministry is called to learn in humility from the tradition of the fathers as expressed by the holy canons. The experience of the Church, also expressed by the holy canons, can help us respond to fundamental issues related to the transmission of truth.

The transmission of truth, which is the Church's tradition, cannot be completely understood externally or rationally. One must experience and know it personally. Only in the communion of faith is an internal and personal familiarity with the truths of the faith, as well as with the teacher of the faith, possible. Only in the communion of faith is the Holy Spirit given so that one can know the truth. That is why every attempt to understand the truth of the gospel from outside will prove futile (see 1 Cor 2.14-16).

The contemporary person often attempts to approach the faith rationally, as an ideology, and is therefore unable truly to understand it. Ecclesiastical experience is the only way to know the truth. For this reason, it is essential for the Church's pastors to help the members of their flock, especially those with problems of faith, to acquire this experience mainly in the liturgical-eucharistic life of the Church. It is there that the Church reveals and at the same time realizes her true divine-human nature.

Integrated into the tradition of the Church, the believer is thereby integrated as well into her life and her truth, which is a hypostatic truth, the incarnate Word of God. This, too, is why Orthodox pastoral ministry presupposes the acceptance of tradition as a necessary condition for spiritual growth. The believing Christian approaches tradition as a learner and not as a teacher. He allows himself to be molded within it rather than to mold it to his own dimensions. He then discovers that tradition is a source of life having an unfathomable depth. Drawing from such an unfathomable depth, he can then render the word of the Church relevant and salutary in every age.

The Role of the Holy Canons[13]

Although the holy canons constitute the Church's law, they nevertheless differ essentially from all other types of law. Even though they are endowed with technical and juridicial articulation, their basis is theological and their objective is pastoral. They were enacted in response to specific pastoral needs of the Church. Furthermore, they express in time her eternal truth, as well as her divine-human will. As such, they cannot be distinguished into canons of divine law and those of human ecclesiastical law, since everything that takes place in the Church is due to the synergy of both divine and human factors.[14]

The redemptive mission of the Church has as a corollary the redemptive and pastoral purpose of all her functions and decrees. Everything that takes place in the Church has as its purpose the salvation of humankind and is pastoral. It is impossible, therefore, for pastoral theology and soteriology (the study of the redemptive mission of the Church) to be distinguished.

It is in this spirit that the holy canons should be understood. The Church's canons are first and foremost pastoral texts, i.e., texts written to regulate specific needs of the Church as a communion of believers or to guide the spiritual life of each of her members.[15] Every canon presupposes a specific pastoral problem, which the Church confronts in a special pastoral way summarized and concretized in a corresponding canon.

The canons, then, are not the expression of a legalistic spirit, which tends to envelop everything in regulations and to reduce the life of the spirit to juridical norms. They are the expression of the Church's pastoral concern for the salvation of her members.[16] This understanding of the canons on the part of the Church's conscience is supported by the following:

1) The relatively small number of canons issued by the synods, especially the ecumenical synods. In other words, the Church was not transformed into a workshop to devise legal rules and regulations. She formulated canons according to circumstances in order to regulate her affairs whenever there was danger of adulterating her life. In fact, what occurred with the dogmas of the Church also occurred with the canons. Both the dogmas and the canons were formulated sparingly, only when the truth of the Church was in danger of distortions of either a theoretical or practical nature.

2) The absence until now in the Orthodox Church of a codification of the canons comparable to the Code of Canon Law of the Roman Catholic Church.

3) The incidental expression of an opinion by the fathers with regard to contemporary pastoral problems, later recognized as having canonical authority. Many of the canons of the fathers ratified by canon 2 of the Sixth Ecumenical Synod were formulated as responses to questions put to them regarding a variety of pastoral problems. Subsequently, their responses were recognized as canons because of the authority these same fathers enjoyed in the conscience of the Church. For the same reason, excerpts from the written works of the fathers were also included thereafter in the collections of the canons.[17]

4) The authority and exalted status accorded by the conscience of the Church to those fathers who were canonists, theologians, pastors and teachers of the life in Christ. Included among them are St. Basil, St. Athanasios, St. Cyril of Alexandria and St. Gregory of Nyssa.

5) The trust with which the body of the Church has always looked upon the holy canons, never considering them an unbearable burden, but a staff for the Church on her way to the kingdom. The grievances levied against the canons are, it appears, a contemporary phenomenon due either to their misinterpretation or to the adoption by some theologians of criteria totally at variance with the criteria which the Church has always maintained.

The fathers of the Seventh Ecumenical Synod expressing the universal conviction of the Church in their first canon, spoke in a unique way about the holy canons: "For those who have received the priestly dignity, the patterns of the canonical constitutions are both testimonies and instructions, which we, gladly receiving, chant with the divinely inspired David to God the Master, saying: 'I have rejoiced in the way of thy testimonies, as much as in all riches (Ps. 119:14),' and 'Thou hast commanded thy testimonies in righteousness forever (Ps. 119:138).' 'Give me understanding, and I shall live (Ps. 119:144).' And if the prophetic voice commands us to keep the testimonies of God forever and to live by them, it is evident that they must abide unshaken and undisturbed. And also Moses, the seer of God, speaks thus: 'To them nothing is to be added, and from them nothing is to be taken away (Dt. 12:32).' And the divine Apostle, boasting in them cries out, 'things into which angels long to look (1 Pet. 1:12).' And Paul says, 'Even if we, or an angel from heaven, preach unto you any other gospel than what ye have received, let him be anathema (Gal. 1:8).'"[18]

The holy canons, just as God's testimonies, are riches and no one is permitted to add to them or delete from them. This absolute stand of the fathers, often incomprehensible to the contemporary Christian influenced by the currents of secularism, is explained only by the faith of the fathers in the perpetual activity of the Holy Spirit in the Church.

The fact that this synod decreed only twenty-two canons assures us that whatever was said above was in reference to the spirit of the canons, not to their letter. The synod can issue new canons; however, they must not vary from the spirit of earlier canons, that is to say, from the spirit of Catholic Orthodoxy.

The canons regulating the pastoral ministry of the Church, even though directed towards practical pastoral goals, have a theological foundation. They are not to be understood as legal regulations, but as the practical application of the Church's dogmas. Let us use as an example canon 34 of the Holy Apostles, which speaks about the synodal structure of provinces headed by a metropolitan: "...and God will be glorified through the Lord in the Holy Spirit, the Father, and the Son, and the Holy Spirit".[19] In other words, by comparing the Church's synodal structure to the community of persons in the Holy Trinity, the canon here reveals the Church as a reflection of the Holy Trinity.

The cooperation (synergy) of divine and human factors in the synods reveals the mystery of the

Church to be the mystery of divine-human (i.e., theanthropic) communion. The Church speaks as a theanthropic body, and the holy canons express in place and time the Church's theanthropic will and character. This is why canon 19 of Sardica can state what in another context might appear at the very least presumptuous: "These things wholesomely, duly, and fitly decreed, in the estimation of us the bishops, such as are pleasing both to God and to man...".[20]

Within the canonical tradition of the Orthodox Church, the holy canons are not the basis of the Church's formation, but are derived from her following her formation. The Church was not established as a legal institution eventually filled with the grace of the Holy Spirit, but was formed as the mystery of theanthropic communion in Christ through the incarnation of the Logos. The canons exist to preserve that mystery. In that sense, the relationship of the Church to her canonical order is a relationship of essence to form. The form, however, is necessary to give expression to the essence.

The theological character of the canons is what renders them not only different from, but also superior to, secular law. This permits the Church to regulate her pastoral concerns based not upon humanistic principles or religious ideology or even ecclesiastical bureaucracy, but upon the word of God ever present in the Church. Replacing the canons with decisions of the individual will of the Church's shepherds, her bishops, is the equivalent of replacing the theanthropic will of the Church with man's fallen human will. Such replacement will be weak, therefore, and incapable of expressing in time and place the catholic truth of the Church.

The holy canons give testimony to the reality of the Church as a theanthropic communion, historically realized by the presence of the Holy Spirit, far removed from every idealistic view of the Church. As a result, only those who deny the perpetual incarnation of the Church in history, overcome by a kind of ecclesiological monophysitism, could deny the holy canons.[21] Such persons exercise a theology devoid of pastoral experience and are therefore unaware of the reality of the human element in the Church, which must be pastored and transformed into the kingdom of God. The Church, which lives her theology, formulates canons which express her theology, i.e., her truth.

The Concepts of Order and Freedom in Christ[22]

The canons speak about "ecclesiastical order,"[23] "canonical order"[24] or simply "order".[25] This raises the question as to whether it is possible to deny canonical order in the Church in the name of freedom in Christ. Does the Church's law constitute a new burden for the person of grace? Certainly not, for canonical order does not confine freedom in Christ; it insures it. Whenever the holy canons are observed, the human passions, which obstruct the life of freedom, are confined. In other words, a correct response to the question regarding the possible obstruction of freedom in Christ by canonical order presupposes an Orthodox perspective of freedom.

What is the nature and character of freedom in Christ? Freedom in Christ does not consist in the possibility of selfishly projecting our own will. It is the restoration of a communion of true love between God and humankind in Christ by rejecting our own will. Thus, freedom in Christ consists mainly in freedom from the depraved love of self and subjugation by the passions. It is the realization of our true self in proper relationship with God and fellow human beings. As a result, freedom in Christ presupposes love and has as a consequence the restoration of an authentic theanthropic communion of persons.

The holy canons help fallen humanity remain united and in a harmonious relationship with one another in the Church. They do not deprive a person of one's freedom, but rather help one to live that freedom. The canons indicate to the faithful the Church's limits, beyond which there is only outer darkness. They regulate the relations among her various charismatic ministries and orders, so that all may work harmoniously for the increase of the one body of Christ. They also prescribe the appropriate method for those who injure the body and fall away from the Christian faith.

The canons have no power to save by themselves. They help a person, however, to remain in the Church united with the other members of the body, so that one can continue to work out his salvation. The canons as limits do not exhaust the great mystery which is the Church; but without them, the Church cannot be expressed as a communion of love, as God-given order and unity, as the harmonious body of Christ.

There is no contradiction between the work of the Spirit on the one hand and church order on the other, or between the Church as charismatic communion and as institution. The Holy Spirit renders the Church a body, which, of course, means an organization with a structure and order, not disorder and utter chaos.

The Holy Spirit builds up the body as a whole and not simply as an individual part of the body. This means that the Spirit is the life of the whole body and that therefore the various functions and members of the body are in a state of mutual dependence upon one another. The laws of the Spirit in the Church are the criteria according to which the mutual dependence of the various functions and ministries of the body of Christ is realized.

When the members of the Church, pastors or flock, prove themselves unworthy of the gifts of the Holy Spirit and reject its activity, they fall into disorder, discord, factions and utter chaos. In such a state there is "freedom," but not in the Christian sense of the word. Each person acts according to his own feeble will, falling victim to the passions and thereby losing the possibility of freedom in Christ and the attainment of God's kingdom. Such a situation points to the need for the holy canons, which, when applied properly, assist in the realization of true freedom.

In the words of St. Nikodemos of the Holy Mountain: "Deprive material creation of the laws of nature, and its orderliness is at once abolished; and with the abolition of order, the whole universe vanishes. Deprive the Church of the holy canons, and disorder at once intrudes; and as a result of the disorder all her sacred adornment disappears."[26]

Worthy of note is the fact that the rejection of canonical order leads to the opposite of the desired result, i.e., the imposition of the human element upon the divine. What needs to be understood is the fact that despite the steadfastness of the Orthodox Church in her canonical tradition, there are still those in her fold whose degenerate will scorns the theanthropic will of the Church as expressed by the holy canons. Furthermore, their own selfish will seeks to settle ecclesiastical matters without the canons or to distort them for their own calculated motives. In the words of canon 10 of the Synod of Constantinople (861): "Those who appear to be victims of their own passions not only do not shudder at the thought of the punishment provided by the holy canons, but have actually dared to scorn them. For they distort them, and in conformity with their malicious nature make pretense of their will; so that in keeping with the magnitude of their malice, according to St. Gregory the Theologian, not only is what is evil not attributed to them, but is even thought of as good."[27]

Characteristic of the spirit of freedom expressed by the canons are decrees, as well, which give testimony to the fact that the canons surpass the spirit of their time, a spirit which is entirely unaware of political freedom, rights and the equality of all, as understood by society today. Thus, as expressed by canon 8 of St. Nicephorus the Confessor (9th century): "Children born of a concubine, or of persons married a second or third time, though with the provision that they be worthy of holy orders, and have lived a life worthy thereof, may be ordained to the priesthood."[28] Similarly, canon 108 of the Synod of Carthage (419) decrees: "There has been given a law whereby each and every person may by free choice undertake the exercise of Christianity."[29]

Furthermore, no one in the Church has the right to restrict another person in an irrational way, thereby interfering in his freedom and responsibility before God. In the seventh canonical question addressed to Patriarch Nicholas of Constantinople (11th century), one reads: "If it be supposed that an abbot upon dying has left another abbot in his place and has given him a prohibitive ruling not to depart from that monastery, and that later, being reproved by his own conscience as too weak and feeble to govern the monastery, such successor of that monk has departed, what ought he in consequence to do about that ruling?" The patriarch's response is: "That ruling is an unreasonable one, and on this account is also an impossible one. Hence, the person who has been tied by it will be loosed if he goes to the bishop and explains his predicament."[30]

The Changeability of the Holy Canons[31]

Due to their theological nature, the holy canons are unchangeable and unrenewable in spirit since they express in time the eternal truth and essence of the Church.[32] However, because of their pastoral character they can be supplemented and modified in letter and form under certain conditions. This is possible only with the enactment of new canons by the competent ecclesiastical authority, so that new historical realities can be pastorally addressed. What is never allowed is to change and adjust the dogmatic and ecclesiological basis of the canons. Such an act would be tantamount to abandoning the theanthropic truth and reality of the Church.[33]

The ecumenical synods speak of the divinely inspired character of the canons, a conviction alive in the tradition of Orthodoxy up to the present, as expressed by St. Nikodemos of the Holy Mountain: "This book (the Rudder) is, in effect, holy writ next to sacred scripture, and a testament next to the Old

and New Testaments. Next to the first divinely inspired words, its contents are second divinely
inspired words. This book contains the eternal limits
set by the fathers and the laws which endure forever...
which were decreed by ecumenical and local councils through the Holy Spirit... This book is indeed, as
we have called it, the Rudder of the Catholic Church,
which when steered by it securely, directs its passen-
gers, both clergy and laity, to the safe harbor of the
kingdom above. This book is the fruit and the result
and the purpose for which so many... patriarchs labored, so many God-bearing and Spirit-bearing
hierarchs from the ends of the universe journeyed (often when they were both old and ill) and convened
ecumenical and local councils and labored for so
many years."[34]

In view of the genuine Orthodox conviction ar-
ticulated earlier regarding the possibility of changing
the holy canons, the extreme positions taken on this
subject can only be characterized as distortions. On
the one extreme is the position calling for the enactment of new canons contrary in spirit to the earlier
ones, and on the other that calling for the preservation of even the letter of the canons to address
contemporary pastoral needs.[35]

Although these two extreme positions oppose
each other, they nevertheless have one thing in common. They both render pastoral ministry for the
contemporary person inconsequential. Both positions
are based upon a non-Orthodox ecclesiology. According to the first, the transmitted faith cannot transform
the contemporary world. What is sought is the transformation of the Church by the world, rather than
the world by the Church, as she has been handed

down to us in history. According to the second position, the Church of the past cannot meet and transform the contemporary world, because she must retain the old historic forms regardless of new historic conditions. That which takes precedence is the preservation and retention of the letter.

Nevertheless, every genuine pastoral accomodation and renewal of our canonical tradition necessitates besides the correct interpretation of the canons the following presuppositions as well:

1) The element of historical change, due to which change in the canons is also necessary, ought not to be overstressed. It is true that in the modern world drastic changes are taking place, because of which there are changes in the psychology, behavior and general disposition of contemporary society. In reaction, there are those overcome by deep anxiety who call for immediate change in some of the fundamental tenets of the faith, which, if realized, can only lead to the transformation of its essence. Nevertheless, there is much that still remains unchanged, due basically to the unchangeable nature of persons and their existential needs. But even in those situations where there is change, there exists the principle of analogy. Accordingly, the solution given by the canons for certain pastoral problems of the past can be given for other parallel problems of today when analogies are kept. This is the case, for example, in the instance of those converting to Orthodoxy from heresy.[36]

2) The call for change in the canons can also conceivably be used as an excuse for changing the dogmatic truth of the canons. It is perfectly possible that liberal theologians not recognizing the claim of the Orthodox Church to be the One, Holy, Catholic,

and Apostolic Church might call for change in the form of those canons which prohibit the equalization of our Church with all other Christian Churches. Such change would, of course, presuppose variation in the dogmatic basis of these canons as well.

3) The adaptation of the form of the canons to today's needs ought not to occur at the expense of the moral demands of the gospel or of the ascetical ethos of Orthodoxy. The intrusion of a humanistic, anthropocentric spirit in the life of many within the Church causes them to seek forms of pastoral intervention which do not presuppose repentance and struggle for denial of one's old self. Instead, they desire Christianity to attain a kind of secularized, cultural and ideological format, adapted to today's pragmatistic and materialistic values.

4) The undertaking of such an initiative rests with the only competent authority able to realize it, namely an ecumenical synod. Only a true ecumenical synod is able to speak as the conscience of the Church and to exercise creativity from a canonical perspective. It alone can modify canons of earlier synods, providing there are specific pastoral needs requiring it, and under the presuppositions stated above. In the meantime, local synods can decide on matters of local importance through decisions which do not conflict with practices of universal validity within Orthodoxy.

Under these presuppositions, an adaptation and reform, as well as an enactment of new canons is possible for a redemptive encounter of the Church with the world of today. Reform without the above presuppositions may make pastoral ministry contemporary, without however making it relevant to redemption. Only what redeems the world is truly relevant.

It is true that in order for those exercising pastoral ministry to apply the canons correctly, they must experience the spirit of the holy canons and the faith generally of the Church in a profound way. Only then is it possible to understand the importance of the holy canons for contemporary pastoral ministry, so that the appropriate economy may be exercised, whenever necessary, and the corresponding adjustments made for contemporary pastoral problems. A superficial knowledge of the canons is dangerous and can lead either to their rejection or to a legalistic interpretation of spiritual life.

The pastor who has been shaped by the spirit of our tradition, an integral part of which are the holy canons, senses with the guidance of the Holy Spirit how to apply them correctly. The difficulty is not so much that the canons are an anachronism as it is that we are unable to live according to their spirit, which is the spirit of our Orthodox tradition. As a result, the presuppositions and criteria for their correct appropriation are lacking. Therefore, every attempt to change the canons on the part of pastors and theologians who do not live the tradition, is destined to fail. That which is urgently needed is what the fathers call "kale alloiosis" (proper change) of the pastor in the light of tradition, which alone will create the presuppositions for a genuine and authentic renewal of our canonical tradition.[37]

CHAPTER THREE

PASTORAL ISSUES OF CANONICAL TRADITION

The Relationship of Clergy and Laity[38]

Clergy

Clergy are those ordained and appointed to exercise pastoral ministry. These include bishops and presbyters, and deacons, who serve the bishops and presbyters. They do not constitute their own priesthood, but share in Christ's priesthood, being images and types of Christ, who is the true high priest. The distinction between clery and laity is not ontological but liturgical, each order offering service to the Church according to the gift given to it. The clergy have received the gift of shepherding, and so must live irreproachably so as to be an example to the flock. The laity bear witness to the truth of the Church through the presence of Christ in their lives.

Laity

The issue of the laity's participation in the teaching and governing ministries of the clergy ought not to be raised in a superficial way, by simply calling attention to the rights granted the laity by the clergy to teach and preach the divine word or to co-administer the affairs of the Church. Rather, the issue to be raised ought to be if and to what degree the body of the Church exercises the solemn function of witnessing to the Orthodox faith in a charismatic way.

Keeping the conscience of the Church body vigilant and sensitizing it to this function is the best diakonia the Church's pastors can offer the people of God. Unfortunately, the spiritual gift of witness remains for the most part inactive and unused today. A moralistic pastoral theology, without a doctrinal and theological basis, does not contribute to a theological awakening of the Orthodox faithful. The distance between theology and pastoral ministry is undoubtedly responsible for the weak theological sensitivity of both pastors and flock in the Church. Likewise, our remoteness from the monastic tradition contributes to the inertia of the church body's witness, inasmuch as the monks were always the charismatic witnesses of the Church's conscience because of their discernment and release from the passions. A return to the pastoral ministry and theology of the fathers, whose pastoral ministry was theological and whose theology was pastoral, as well as a revival of monastic life, will contribute significantly to the activation of the gift of a dynamic witness by the people of God.[39]

The Synodal Structure of the Church[40]

When exercising pastoral ministry, the clergy must act "synodically," i.e., their whole attitude and pastoral method must express the synodal nature and practice of the Church. The concept of conciliarity, i.e., the conciliar or synodal approach to handling the affairs of the Church, is not confined solely to convening various types of synods, but also includes every expression of ecclesiastical life and pastoral ministry. Through conciliarity, the nature of the

Church as the theanthropic communion in Christ is expressed. This is why any pastoral practice which does not result from conciliarity is a deviation from the Orthodox teaching about the Church.

Besides the convening of synods, the synodal expression of ecclesiastical life is to be found in every act of communion, e.g., first and foremost, among bishops who are the heads of the local (autocephalous) churches, as a way of witnessing to the communion among them; also, in every act of communion between the primate/metropolitan (first ranking bishop) and the bishops under his authority, between the bishop and his presbytery, between the presbyter ("proistamenos") of a community and the fellow clergy and laity comprising it, and finally in acts of communion of the laity among themselves.

At all levels the Church functions as synod, i.e., as a community of persons freely gathered in Christ and by him, so that each may offer his gift for the building up of the body in love. Within Orthodoxy the person is neither absorbed nor identified with the masses. Fellowship with Christ and his assigned shepherds does not cause one to lose one's individuality, but to come alive through communion with him and one's fellow believers.

That is why conciliarity, as a way of life of the Church, is directly related to pastoral ministry. It seeks to fashion ecclesiastical life in such a way as to express faithfully the essence and the ethos of the Orthodox Church.[41] The Church's synodal way of life, which reaches its highest point in the episcopal synods, gives witness to the synergy of God and human beings for the realization of salvation and the endurance of truth. Synods experience the mystery of synergy intensely and establish their work upon this mystery. The experience of those who make up the synods is that they cooperate with God in the formulation and safeguarding of the Church's truth. If the Spirit does not move, human effort and industry alone cannot complete the approximation of the mystery of divine truth, as stated by canon 66 of Carthage: "Then when all things had been considered and treated of which seem to conduce to the advantage of the church, the Spirit of God suggesting and admonishing us, we determined to act leniently and pacifically with the before-mentioned men, ..."[42]

It is, of course, true that although the Church at her core is always synod (the literal meaning of the word "Ekklesia"), her members, both clergy and laity, sometimes fail, because of their spiritual immaturity and sinfulness, to live in harmony with the synodal character of the Church. They fail to express in their pastoral ministry and in their relationships her synodal spirit. We have an anti-synodal spirit and ethos, for example, when the convocation of synods is postponed or frustrated so that the authority of one person or group of hierarchs may be imposed upon the rest; or when synods are convened, however without the possibility of free discussion and decision on the part of those in attendance.

Within the concept of true communion is understood cooperation, mutual respect and recognition of the God-given worth and gifts with which each member, and especially each pastor, of the Church is endowed. This understanding of communion stands totally opposed to attempts on the part of strong minority factions to impose their will upon a synod, or to stifle their adversaries. Such activity does not allow for a free and open synodal discussion to determine truth and to express what constitutes common ecclesiastical conscience. Everyone must hear prayerfully, attentively and respectfully what his fellow Christian has to say, providing, of course, he has not fallen into obvious heresy. Only by listening with humility is discussion, agreement and obedience of all in Christ possible.

It is a great sin against the body of Christ to attempt to remove the synodal approach to resolving issues in the Church. This betrays a lack of trust in the gifts with which all the living members of the Church have been endowed.

It is quite possible for a bishop to administer his diocese contrary to synodal practice. He might use fear as a means of imposing his will and not love, or blind military discipline and not obedience in Christ. In such a case, the bishop, considering himself to be the sole possessor of spiritual gifts in the diocese, rejects the gifts of both clergy and laity under his authority. Instead of one who coordinates and is the center of unity of all those with spiritual gifts, he becomes their captor. To such a bishop, the venerable presbytery are not "the bishop's counselors and the Church's crown," as they are called in the Apostolic Constitutions,[43] but the executive officers of his commands. Such being the case, the presbyters do not co-administer and co-pastor together with the bishop. Instead, they are reduced to a kind of employee, who executes the orders of his superior, formally and studiously perhaps, however without personal participation and zeal. Presbyters accustomed to such impersonal ecclesiastical bureaucracy often become impersonal bureaucrats themselves.

Similarly, it is quite possible for a presbyter to administer the affairs of his parish in the same anti-synodal, "despotic" way. The pastor who administers his parish synodically will afford the opportunity to all members of his community to offer their gifts for the building up of the body. Pastors and flock in every parish can realize in their lives the Church's truth in a communion of faith and love. Truth is not something which the pastor offers and which the flock accepts passively. Rather, it is the gift of God in which pastor and flock commune in unity, with the guidance and leadership, of course, of the pastor.

In those situations when the head believes it can achieve all things without the cooperation of the other members of the body, it is natural that there will be a lack of development not only of the body, but also of the head.

The synodal exercise of pastoral responsibilities does not lead, as some fear, to a decline in ecclesiastical order, but actually contributes to its increase. When the pastor of a community works together with those around him for the maintenance of ecclesiastical order, he appoints his co-workers to be the guardians of this order. He thus achieves his goal through the open contribution of all – both pastors and flock.

The conciliarity of the Church is likewise weakened whenever her members create groups and factions, as in the Church of Corinth (1 Cor 12.12-13). Such exclusivism only causes these persons to consider other members of the body less united to them than the members of their own faction. Sometimes they even refuse to cooperate with the canonical pastor in their parish or bishop in their diocese.

In order to overcome a lack of conciliarity, which betrays an egocentric, non-transfigured life in Christ, repentance and transformation of the inner person are necessary. This alone makes possible living the mystery of the Church in truth, i.e., in a catholic and synodal way. The struggle of those who are vigilant and who experience theologically the mystery of the Church is always clear: only through repentance is synodal life and management of the Church's affairs possible.[44]

The Problem of Sin[45]

The Nature of Sin

Another basic topic with which Orthodox pastoral ministry concerns itself is healing the person plagued by sin. Sin is a disease which causes spiritual death in a person. Indeed, it separates him from God, the source of life. The only cure for sin is sincere repentance, which is cultivated through penances (epitimia). Penances have a therapeutic, not legalistic, character and are imposed in accordance with certain principles which stem from the holy canons.

The canons do not make the scholastic distinction between mortal and non-mortal sins, in view of the fact that such a distinction includes the danger of a moralistic and legalistic approach to sin. "Mortal sin" is the denial of repentance. In the words of canon 5 of the Seventh Ecumenical Synod: "It is a sin unto death, when some, having sinned, remain without correction; but it is still worse, when men, proudly lifting their necks, rise against piety and truth, preferring mammon to the obedience of God, and not clinging to His canonical precepts."[46]

As for the causes of sin, one might apply generally what is said with reference to denial of Christ during the period of the persecutions. Such denial specifically, and all sin generally, is due to "weakness of the flesh,"[47] which having been adversely affected because of original sin, leans towards evil. Another cause is "lack of strength," as well as "cowardice and fear".[48] On the other hand, there are persons overcome by sin because of the "great violence of the evil scheming devil".[49]

The canons urge that these causes always be kept in mind when assessing the degree of responsibility of the sinner and when determining the appropriate therapy. Sin, most of the time, generates other sins, which afflict not only the sinner, but also the other members of the Church. The sinfulness especially of the Church's pastors may as a direct result contribute to agitation among the laity. A bishop, for example, moved by greed or ambition, who aspires to be transferred to a larger diocese, might cunningly invite the laity to support him.[50]

The canons distinguish between sins voluntary and involuntary, known and unknown. Sins committed freely and wittingly by a person, e.g., are considered more serious than those not committed under those circumstances.

Determining the degree to which a person willingly participated in committing a sin is most important for determining the appropriate penance (epitimion), certainly not as retribution but as therapy. Sin committed willingly and wittingly and without force or need indicates a more serious spiritual malady, which needs a longer period of therapy through penance.

A sin committed unwittingly lessens the sinner's degree of responsibility; however, it is not granted amnesty, neither is it considered as never having taken place. Thus, if the unwitting sinner is a priest, he may not exercise his priesthood, but only retain the honor of his priestly office. Such, e.g., is the case with the presbyter engaged in an illicit marriage.[51]

Sin and the Passions

The canons know only one means of healing the sick person from sin – sincere repentance. The condition for repentance is humility, distress of heart, and seeking God's forgiveness. The pastor must discern whether the repentance is truly sincere before receiving those cut off from the Church because of their sins (especially heresy), even if on their death bed.

A sure criterion of repentance is the non-repetition of offenses. This can only be achieved by practicing "askesis" to acquire the opposite virtue to every sin. In order for the health of the soul to be restored, it is necessary for the penitent not only to be guided in ceasing to do evil, but also to be actively engaged in doing the corresponding good.

The pastor must guide the penitent to do real penance, which is to say to restore what was lost by sin. As long as the penitent continues to be bound by sin, he cannot be received into ecclesiastical communion. He who repents is fully restored to the Church, no matter how serious the sin.[52] The justification of the penitent Christian is due to the grace of God through the work of Christ and not to the penitent's good works as means of self-justification. It is on this point that Christian justification differs essentially from all other non-Christian concepts of justification, including that of classical Greek philosophy.

Besides healing from sin, pastoral ministry must also concern itself with its prevention. Pastors are called upon first of all to urge their spiritual children to distance themselves from all temptation, even martyrdom.[53] The spiritual flock must also be taught to avoid the root, i.e., the cause, of sin and to pay attention even to one's thoughts, out of which emanate one's acts.[54]

Many canonical prohibitions aim at protecting the faithful from the causes of sin. Characteristic of this is canon 100 of the Sixth Ecumenical Synod, which prohibits indecent images: "'Let your eyes look directly forward,' and 'keep your heart with all vigilance,' orders Wisdom (Prov. 4:25, 23). For the senses of the body easily bring their own impressions into the soul. Therefore we order that from now on there shall in no way whatsoever be made pictures, whether they be in paintings or in any other way, which bewitch the eye and corrupt the mind, and incite it to the enkindling of base pleasures. And if anyone shall attempt to do this, let him be excommunicated."[55]

The pastor must always be vigilant about the salvation of his flock. He must never reconcile himself to sin. Even his tolerance of incorrigible sinners makes him a companion to their sin.[56]

It is to be understood that severe measures should only be taken after all possible mild measures have first been exhausted. E.g., those who establish an illicit assembly in defiance of their own bishop are to be deposed if they are clergymen and excommunicated if laymen. This, however, is to take place only after a "first and second and third plea of the bishop" goes unheeded.[57] The use of the word for plea ("paraklesis") is strongly suggestive of the paternal approach of the bishop.

The event of sin is seen by the holy canons in an ecclesiological context, not in an individualistic one. Sin separates the sinner not only from God, but also from the children of God, the members of the body of Christ, whom the sinner directly or indirectly offends. Only from this perspective are we able to understand why the sinner is cut off from the ecclesiastical gathering and ecclesiological mystery of the holy eucharist. It is also for this reason that the penitent confesses his sins to a representative of the church community. In the early Church, confession was a public practice.

The bishop and presbyter, as icons of Christ who preside over the eucharistic gatherings, have also received from God the authority to "loose and bind".[58] Consequently, it is they who receive the repentance of the sinner and who are obliged to restore the sinner to the body of the Church.[59] The restoration is realized by degrees through penances, as often as the condition of the penitent warrants. In the early practice of the Church, the entire body of the faithful suffered in common with the penitents and prayed for them as often as their sin was known, as in the case of lapsed Christians who later repented.[60]

Revealing one's sin privately "to the priest through confession"[61] does not mean that the mystery is reduced from its ecclesiological character to a personal event. The confessor priest is always he who presides at the eucharistic assembly of the ecclesiastical community (parish), to which he reconciles the penitent. Nevertheless, replacing public confession with private confession may give the impression that it is a personal event. For this reason, pastors must teach their spiritual flock about the ecclesiological dimension of the mystery of penance as well.

Penances ("Epitimia") and Their Therapeutic Character

Penances in the Eastern Church have always had a spiritual character. Furthermore, the use of physical force of any kind is strictly forbidden.[62] For every type of penance applied there are certain principles determined by the holy canons which the pastor must always bear in mind.

1) Penances always have a therapeutic and pastoral- pedagogical character, never judicial, neither do they constitute a means to satisfy divine justice.

2) Because of the therapeutic character of penances when they are applied, not only is the seriousness of the sin and the length of abstention from holy communion taken into account, but also the sincerity of the penitent's repentance and his predisposition. Voluntary confession is a sign of sincere repentance and ought therefore to be considered in dealing more leniently with the penitent.

3) The therapeutic character of penances is also attested to by the possibility afforded by the holy canons to adjust their length of time while being practiced. The decisive factor in their adjustment is the sincerity with which penance is performed. On this issue there is wide agreement among the canons.

4) There are also other factors to be considered with regard to imposing penances:

a) The age and marital status of the sinner, whether married or celibate. In the case of carnal sin, persons under age 20 are penanced more leniently than those over 20, as are celibates as opposed to married persons.[63]

b) The frequency of the sin, i.e., whether it was committed once or repeatedly.[64]

c) The status or order of the sinner in the Church.[65] A clergyman, for example, who falls into sin is dealt with more harshly than a layman.

d) The general state of the members of the Church from the perspective of faith and morals. When faith is stronger and the Church more firmly established, then the penances imposed ought to be more strict.[66]

e) The spiritual condition and psychosynthesis of the penitent ought also to be seriously considered when giving penances. The canons speak about "appropriate penances".[67] What they are referring to is the principle of "individualization" ("exatomikefsis"), known as well in psychology and pedagogics, and profusely invoked in the pastoral theology of the fathers. This is in view of the fact that each member of the body is distinguishable by the different characteristics of his personality.[68]

This principle, which is so important to pastoral theology, is also invoked by canon 102 of the Sixth Ecumenical Synod: "It is incumbent upon those who have received from God the power to loose and bind, to look into the quality of the sin and the readiness of the sinner for conversion, and to apply medicine suitable for the disease, lest by using the improper measure for either he should fail in regard to the healing of the sick man. For the disease of sin is not simple, but varied and multiform, and it germinates many mischievous offshoots, from which evil is diffused for a long time, and it proceeds further until it is stopped by the power of the physician. Therefore, he who professes the science of spiritual medicine ought first of all consider the disposition of him who has sinned, and to see whether he tends to health or, on the contrary, invites to himself disease by his own behavior, and to observe how he can care for his manner of life during the interval. And if he does not oppose the physician, and if the ulcer of the soul grows by the application of the medicaments thereon, then let him grant him mercy according to his worth. For the whole account is between God and him to whom the pastoral rule has been delivered, to lead back the wandering sheep and to cure that which is wounded by the serpent; and that he may neither push them down to the precipices of despair, nor loosen the bridle towards dissolution or contempt of life; but in some way at any rate, either by means of more stern and astringent, or by more gentle and mild medicines, to resist this sickness and exert himself for the healing of the ulcer, now examining the fruits of his repentance and wisely managing the man who is called to higher illumination. Moreover, we ought to know two things, both the things which belong to strictness and those which belong to custom, and to follow, as holy Basil (canon 3) teaches us, the traditional form in the case of those who are not fitted for the highest things."[69]

A close examination of this canon reveals the following two pastoral principles:

1) For there to be therapy, one must have a spiritual father. The person who is under the influence of sin and the devil cannot heal himself. The selection of penances is at the discretion of the confessor, since they are the means towards attaining salvation. The confessor must, however, choose wisely, relying on the charism of "diakrisis" (discernment), i.e., the capacity granted by the Holy Spirit to perceive correctly the spiritual condition of the penitent and to offer the appropriate therapy. Only pastors with the charism of discernment are able to exercise the ministry of the spiritual father effectively.

2) The penance given must be analogous to the readiness of the penitent to receive it.

The Pastoral Approach to Heresy and Schism[70]

Heresy and schism constitute serious sins which are difficult to be cured. They are means through which the devil tries to prevent a person's salvation by cutting him off from the life-giving communion of the Church.

As reflected in the holy canons, the fathers do not view heresy with tolerance and relativism. They absolutely condemn it as something frightful and odious. This is the same view they hold of schism. Towards heretics, however, they express love, taking all possible measures and making ample use of economy for their repentance. Economy is used for heretics only insofar as they return to the Church, never so long as they remain in heresy.

Despite the distinction between heresy and schism in the consciousness of the Church, both are considered equally destructive in causing a person's separation from the body of Christ.[71]

The cause of schism is pride and arrogance, leading one to separate from the Church and to offer the holy gifts "separately" on other erected altars "contrary to ecclesiastical faith and discipline," in the language of canon 10 of Carthage.[72]

So long as the heretic is deprived of grace, it is not possible for him to retain the identity of a member of the Church. The anathema does not cut him off from the Church. It proclaims to the body that he has cut himself off by falling from the true faith. This it does in the hope of ultimately saving both the heretic and the other members of the body.

Likewise, the schismatic who separates himself from the Church and is deprived of divine grace, is deposed if a clergyman and excommunicated if a layperson. The ecclesiastical penances for the schismatic, as well, recognize the condition in which this person willingly because of his actions finds himself. As stated characteristically in canon 5 of Antioch: "(If) any presbyter or deacon, despising his own bishop, has separated himself from the Church,...."[73]

This canon proposes the method for the return of schismatics. There precede a first and second invitation, then a personal admonishment of the bishop, following which the infliction of deposition is unavoidable.

Finally, the severe position which the canons take towards heretics is in the final analysis compassionate. In the first place, it is to protect the flock from the scourge of heresy; then, too, it is to convey a message to the consciences of the heretics in the hope that they will return to the fold from which they strayed.

Ways to the Kingdom: Marriage and Monasticism[74]

The purpose of the Church's pastoral ministry is to assist the struggling Christian in his journey towards the kingdom. There are two ways to the kingdom, the monastic life and marriage in Christ. Both ways lead to salvation. Both virginity and marriage are good and holy, although virginity, because of its eschatological character, is considered exceptional. The holy canons contain valuable elements referring to the pastoral ministry of monasticism and marriage. It is a basic teaching of the canons and the holy fathers that every Christian, not only the monk, has to live the ascetic life in proportion to the special situation of his life. Ascetic practice (askesis) is a necessary condition for experiencing the Orthodox ethos. That is what elevates a person from his spiritually fallen state to his natural condition ("kata physin"), and from his natural condition to a supernatural state ("hyper physin").

Marriage in Christ

Following are certain fundamental positions with regard to the underlying theology of marriage in the holy canons, which can also be applied to a contemporary pastoral ministry of marriage.

First of all, marriage is considered a personal event. The communion of persons in marriage based upon love is unique and permanent.[75] The uniqueness of marriage is removed by a second or third marriage, which are accepted only by economy and out of compassion for human frailty. This uniqueness, however, is in principle shattered by adultery, as made clear by St. Gregory of Nyssa in his fourth canon. Because it entails denial of love towards one's spouse and is an offense against him/her, it is canonized by this saint with a double penance as opposed to the sin of fornication.

As a personal event, marriage also constitutes a personal right freely accepted by those joined in matrimony. Consequently, abduction is canonized as a serious offence for both abductor and his accomplice(s).[76] Furthermore, he who rapes the woman he later marries is given the penance of a fornicator.[77]

The impediments of marriage due to relationship based on scripture, known also in natural law, do not intend to restrict the right of marriage but to protect it. The prohibition of the marriage of an Orthodox Christian with non-Christians and certain heterodox does not affect the personal character of marriage, since the sacramental basis of marriage presupposes a common faith. This prohibition is explained by the fact that communion with a spouse of another faith cannot be complete, because they share neither faith nor sacraments.

A serious problem is caused today by the great number of divorces, which testifies to the dulling of the sacramental character of marriage in the consciousness of Christians. Instead, marriage is thought of more as a legal act following common consent and not, first and foremost, as a sacred act performed with the grace of the Holy Spirit. The acceptance of marriage as a legal act results in its easy dissolution when cohabitation of the spouses ceases. The Church struggled fiercely during the Byzantine era to introduce a sacramental view of marriage and to abolish divorce by mutual consent. She eventually succeeded with the help of the state, which incorporated into its legislation the theology of the Church.

In spite of the fact that the Church struggled against existing trends in the state to grant an unlimited number of divorces, she nevertheless did not rule out divorce entirely. This was in line with her belief that the permanency of Christian marriage "cannot always be considered intact no matter what, simply because there is a legal confirmation,"[78] or that, "the unity of the spouses cannot be preserved by legal force alone".[79]

The toleration of divorce does not mean that the Church considers the spouses morally unaccountable, especially those spouses who share all or most of the responsibility for the divorce. According to the canons, those entering into a second marriage are under the penance of temporary abstention from holy communion.[80] Also, at the blessing of a second marriage, the priest prays that the Lord will forgive those who because of the weakness of the flesh are entering into the marriage.

In contemporary pastoral practice this sense of a second or third marriage has unfortunately been lost. To this fact should be added the anti-religious spirit which prevails in our age, with the result that the sanctity and uniqueness of marriage are being compromised in the consciousness of the faithful. It is therefore imperative that a pastoral approach towards divorced persons and those marrying a second and third time be applied which is more consistent with the Church's teaching. The imposition of some kind of penance and the avoidance of a formal wedding seem appropriate.

A basic need in today's pastoral approach to marriage in order to preserve it is for the faithful to experience it first and foremost as a relationship "in the Lord," i.e., as a mystery of theanthropic communion, whose dissolution constitutes a very grave sin. Marriage viewed in a secularistic sense, mainly as a social institution and biological event deprived of any sacramental character, does not contribute to the spiritual advancement of the spouses in the Lord and to its preservation. Furthermore, the sacramental view of marriage is hindered by the following factors: the lack of a pastoral, premarital preparation of the spouses; the mere formal granting of the bishop's permission and formal celebration of the service; the insistence upon a religious ceremony even when one of the spouses, a nominal Christian, declares his opposition to the faith; or, finally, the formal issuance of an ecclesiastical divorce to declare that the marriage is dissolved.

In view of all these issues, it behooves us as a Church to re-examine our stand so as to achieve a radical cure to the problems related to marriage within the realm of our canonical and theological tradition. Certainly, a formal and conventional approach to marriage will only contribute to its destruction.

The Monastic Life

The canonical tradition of the Church, echoing the spirit of holy scripture, points to the ascetic character of the monastic as well as of the married life in Christ. This is in view of the fact that all are called to salvation and all must through askesis become "men of violence" ("viastai", Mt 11.12), i.e., they must use violence in subjugating their rebellious nature to do the holy will of God. From this perspective, every genuine Christian must be an ascetic. And although askesis is the common lot of both monks and married Christians alike, there is a difference as to the kind of askesis and how it is to be practiced. The obligation of askesis encumbent upon all Christians prescribes more than anything else a struggle in refraining from the passions.

Fasting as a common obligation and spiritual aid pertains to all Christians except the sick, women who are pregnant, and those who have just given birth, according to the canons. It testifies to the ascetic character of the Christian life and aims at humbling both body and soul.

Fasting and all askesis generally should be practiced according to ecclesiastical tradition. Therefore, clergy and laity who fast on Sunday or Saturday are severely penanced.[81] This is the way in which the unity of the Church is secured, as well as the conquest, in humility, of blind individualism. Following one's own canons with regard to askesis, especially fasting, is hideous arrogance and therefore unsparingly condemned.[82]

Askesis, as projected by the canons, is entirely opposed to platonic or manichaean askesis, which is based upon mistaken theological presuppositions, considering matter and the body as a repository of evil. The body as an inferior element to the soul must be subjected to it, not however punished or despised through askesis. The Church through her canons always condemned such deviations.[83]

The pastoral task of the Church not only has askesis itself in mind, but also the spirit and disposition with which the faithful practice it. The condition of today's world undoubtedly compels the Church's pastors to re-examine the issue of askesis in the light of tradition. The holy canons are especially helpful in accomplishing just that. The first thing they remind us is that askesis constitutes an evangelical command for all the faithful, providing, of course, the proper analogies are kept. Abandonment of the ascetic ethos of Orthodoxy would be in contradiction to the gospel.

The canons remind us also of the possibility of applying economy according to each individual case by the canonically competent ecclesiastical authority. Economy does not abolish the canon, given the extraordinary circumstances in which we live today.

For example, the requirements of the holy canons with regard to fasting ought not to be overlooked by abolishing the traditional fasting period. Spiritual fathers may, however, permit by economy lesser fasts depending upon the condition of the spiritual child, i.e., factors such as health, occupation and age. In this way, the fasting period is not shortened and those striving for spiritual perfection are permitted to run the course, each according to his own strength and zeal.(84) A limitation of the fasting period would deprive those striving for perfection of the possibility for greater askesis. It would also contribute to the slothfulness of the remaining faithful by reducing the spiritual challenge put before them. Moreover, the whole atmosphere within which the Orthodox Church lives (her worship, piety and mysticism) is ascetic and in harmony with the requirements of the canons. Consequently, every attempt at moving away from an Orthodox ascetic ethos would have as a result the corruption of ecclesiastical life in general and secularization of the Church.

EPILOGUE

The pastoral guidance of Christians in today's secular society necessarily presupposes a foundation of inspired principles and methods preserved in the teaching of the One, Holy, Catholic, and Apostolic Orthodox Church of Christ.[85]

Such a foundation is especially necessary in view of our susceptibility to adopt pastoral "techniques" under the influence of various elements alien to ecclesiastical ministry. Through this influence, pastoral ministry as exercised in the Orthodox Church has frequently been deprived of its Christ-centered focus, thereby becoming anthropocentric.[86]

A significant step towards overcoming precisely this vulnerabilty of our pastoral ministry and effecting its return to the spirit, principles and methods of the ancient, undivided Church has already been taken. It is to be found in the effort to correlate pastoral ministry and the rudder of the Church, i.e. the holy canons.

We must focus our attention upon the theory of pastoral ministry, especially its contemporary manifestations, such as pastoral psychology. In order to be certain that contemporary ministry truly incorporates the divine and human (theanthropic) elements of pastoral theology experienced throughout the ages by the One, Holy, Catholic, and Apostolic Church, the body of Christ, it is necessary to study the methods of pastoral theology handed down by the holy fathers.

Today's anthropocentric pastoral ministry developed for the most part in a secular context. Despite its apparent luster on the surface, it remains deficient in essence, without redemptive value, because it is not rooted in the mystery of the Church. It investigates the problems of a person anthropocentrically, i.e., with human criteria and a human method. The soul, which thirsts for union with God, does not rest upon the moral imperatives or psychological analyses of a particular school of psychological thought. It does not even rest upon the human assistance provided by psychiatry.

The shepherd of souls, like Moses of old, must deliver his flock from the bondage of the devil, of sin, and of death to the "glorious liberty of the children of God" (Rom 8.21)[87] and commit to the Lord souls perfected and sanctified. In view of such a task, he must realize the insufficiency of an anthropocentric pastoral ministry. One must therefore turn to the holy canons, which express the experience of the Church as confirmed by the synods and the fathers. Each father is considered the mouth of the Church because of his obedience to her and identification of his will with that of the Lord. The decisions of the synods express to an even greater degree the will of the Church and constitute a certain path of salvation.

In the holy canons is to be found all the pastoral experience and theology of the Church. Whoever wishes to find the most genuine expression, method or experience of pastoral ministry need only turn to the canons. Furthermore, Orthodox pastoral ministry must not be exercised according to each shepherd's subjective view, but according to the will of God, as expressed by holy scripture and tradition and the holy canons based on them. This is why the canons and pastoral theology are so closely bound together. Whoever pastors according to the holy canons, pastors in the spirit of the Church, according to the will of God. He who pastors independently of the holy canons according to his own convictions pastors merely as an individual apart from the Church.

Pastoring with ecclesiastical sensitivity is a question of the salvation of both pastors and faithful. The Church always affirmed her faith in the divine and human natures of Christ by means of the synods and holy fathers. The temptation of offering salvation not through him who was God and Man, but only through man – a human being, was never absent from humankind. That is why today there is pastoral ministry which is Orthodox and encompasses both divine and human elements, and there is also pastoral ministry in various forms, usually hidden, which is concerned mostly with human elements. Such an anthropocentric pastoral ministry denies obedience to the holy canons and tradition of the Church. And under the pretense of bringing pastoral ministry in line with contemporary thinking, such an approach arrogantly projects the will of the unredeemed individual as the regulator of pastoral methodology and moral behavior.

We must, of course, approach the canons in repentance and humility, not to judge them, but to learn pastoral theology and methods of ministry. We ought not to invoke them whenever we want to support our personal interests, while forgetting them whenever they judge our anti-ecclesiastical and uncanonical acts.[88] The hearts of those who sincerely and unselfishly love the Church grieve whenever they ascertain the frequent inconsistencies towards the holy canons.

Those who fault the canons for being outdated or for conflicting with the spirit of Christ's love are also imbued with an anthropocentric spirit. Such a theology is anti-traditional, based upon the mistaken view regarding the discovery of unadulterated Christianity not in the later tradition of the Church, but in the primitive Christianity of the New Testament. All who live the mystery of the Church in an Orthodox ethos know that the Church of the synods is no less the body of Christ or less holy than the primitive Church. Those who are alien to ecclesiastical life and experience and do not live the Church internally and in repentance are unable to comprehend Orthodox canonical tradition. If we do not comprehend the canons, they are not at fault. We, who lack the necessary spiritual vision to see as God sees, are at fault.

All this points to the need to study the holy canons. In doing so, one must search first and foremost for the theological and pastoral elements they contain, remembering that pastoral ministry divorced from theology is reduced to a technique, or to empty moral rules and obligations which have no relation to the theologically grounded pastoral theology of the Church. Moveover, the study of the pastoral and theological nature of the canons provides the opportunity for their correct assessment and appreciation. Through such a study it becomes evident that despite their legal expression the holy canons do indeed have a theological basis and a pastoral purpose.[89]

What is said above about the holy canons comes at a time when there is much confusion about the character and role of the canons in the Church. This sense of confusion is due mainly to the spirit of secularism which pervades our society. It is to be hoped that the present study on the spiritual nature of the holy canons will contribute to a more serious and respectful predisposition towards them and to a more firm grounding of our pastoral ministry in their teachings.[90]

The pastoral ministry of the Church has always been based upon the holy canons, which constitute the Church's law. Nevertheless, the relationship between pastoral ministry and the canons is not always correctly understood. The result is that we are sometimes directed towards antinomianism, which is the autonomous exercise of pastoral ministry in the absence of the canons, and other times towards legalism, i.e., the exercise of pastoral ministry according to the letter of the canons only, in a legalistic, juridical way.

The adoption and application of the holy canons by the Church as her law coincides with the teaching of holy scripture that the law, which is an expression of grace, is a gift of God to His people. It has an instructive and pastoral character, which helps elevate and free the believer in Christ.

When one understands the true character of the law in holy scripture and the relationship between the law and grace, one also correctly understands the relationship between the holy canons and pastoral ministry. Understood in this way, pastoral ministry is protected from the two dangerous extremes of legalism and antinomianism.[91]

An overview of the theology of law in the Old and New Testaments reveals the following conclusions:

1) The law of the Old Testament is not in substance detrimental, even though it is incomplete and temporary. The law has a pastoral and soteriological character. Even the incomplete law of the Old Testament is necessary as a "pedagogue in Christ". As decreed by the 82nd canon of the Sixth Ecumenical Synod: "Therefore, embracing the ancient types, and the shadows, as symbols of the truth and patterns given to the Church, we prefer grace and truth, receiving it as the fulfillment of the law" (Gal 3.19-25).[92]

2) The law is not some beneficial human invention, but an expression of God's revealed will for humankind (Ex 24.12; Lev 24.22).

3) The law is a means and not an end. By applying the law in humility, a person can be elevated to a relationship of love towards God and fellow human beings. In such a relationship one receives divine grace, the life of God, and salvation (1 Tim 1.8-11).

4) Misuse of the law by transforming it from a means to an end becomes spiritually fatal for a person. However, the law is not responsible for its misinterpretation (Rom 7.6-16, 9.30-32).

5) The Lord reveals the true content of the misinterpreted law of the Old Testament and indicates that its true character is to be found in love. Love and decrees of law are in a relationship of substance and form (Mt 22.36-40; Rom 13.8-10).

6) True freedom for the believer is not to be found in discarding the law, which is lawlessness, but in preserving it by living in love as responsible freedom towards God and fellow human beings (Rom 6.15-18; Jas 1.25).

According to the patristic interpretation of scripture, there is no contradiction between law and grace; rather, law constitutes an expression of grace.

Hence, the Church, as the body of Christ and people of God headed towards the kingdom, adopted canons which from the apostolic period served to guide the faithful pastorally on their way. Such a canon, as is well known, was adopted by the so-called apostolic synod in Jerusalem: "For it has seemed good to the Holy Spirit and to us to lay upon you no greater burden than these necessary things: that you abstain from what has been sacrificed to idols and from blood and from what is strangled and from unchastity. If you keep yourselves from these, you will do well. Farewell" (Acts 15.28-29).

Only when one approaches the holy canons with an Orthodox ecclesiastical spirit and humility can one understand their importance for preserving unity and peace in the Church, as well as the correct pastoral guidance for her members. They are thus understood to be a precious gift of the Divine Founder of the Church to both clergy and laity, for which the words of the holy fathers of the Seventh Ecumenical Synod referred to earlier (canon 1) take on special meaning: "Gladly receiving (the holy canons), (we) chant with the divinely inspired David to God the Master, saying: 'I have rejoiced in the way of thy testimonies, as much as in all riches,' (Ps. 119:14) and 'Thou hast commanded thy testimonies in righteousness forever.' (Ps. 119:138) 'Give me understanding, and I shall live (Ps. 119:144).'"[93]

NOTES

* With the exception of the Introduction, this volume is an adaptation in translation of the excellent study on the subject of the pastoral dimension of the holy canons by the Very Reverend Archimandrite George Kapsanis, Abbot of the Monastery Grigoriou on Mount Athos [*He poimantike diakonia kata tous hierous kanonas* {"Pastoral Ministry according to the Holy Canons"}, (Piraeus, 1976)]. As an abridgement, it includes only those parts which are especially germane to the issue of the pastoral nature of canonical tradition. It is mostly a translation; however, some sections are a free rendering of the original and appear elsewhere as well. In the opinion of this translator and editor, it offers valuable insights to the proper understanding of Orthodox canonical tradition.

[1] See R. Metz, *What is Canon Law?*, (London: Burnes and Oates, 1960), 12-17.

[2] *Kanon* I (Vienna, 1973), 45-53.

[3] Archondonis, "A Common Code," p. 48.

[4] J. Meyendorff, "Contemporary Problems of Orthodox Canon Law," *Greek Orthodox Theological Review* 17 (1972), 41.

[5] *St. Vladimir's Seminary Quarterly* 11 (1967), 54-68.

[6] Afanasiev, "The Canons," p. 60.

[7] Afanasiev, p. 63.

[8] Canonical texts other than canons of the ecumenical synods, with some exceptions, are taken from H. Percival, ed., *The Seven Ecumenical Councils*, vol. 14 of *Nicene and Post-*

Nicene Fathers, second series (Grand Rapids, MI: Eerdmans, 1956), (hereafter, Percival, The Seven). Occasionally, I have used my own translation for specific words and phrases.

[9] See L. Patsavos, "Lived Experience and Theoretical Differences in the Approach to Law and Discipline in the Eastern and Western Churches," *Rightly Teaching the Word of Your Truth*, ed. by N. Vaporis, (Brookline, MA: Holy Cross Orthodox Press, 1995), 187-9.

[10] Kapsanis, *He Poimantike*, 37-47.

[11] Cf. L. Patsavos, "Ecclesiastical Reform: At What Cost?," *Greek Orthodox Theological Review* 40 (1-2), 1995, published together with other papers delivered at the international conference commemorating the 1300th anniversary of the Council "in Trullo" at Holy Cross School of Theology (March 1992). The theme of the conference, ecclesiastical reform, is developed at length from the perspective of Orthodox canonical tradition.

[12] Kapsanis, *He Poimantike*, 49-57.

[13] Kapsanis, 59-71.

[14] See Afanasiev, "The Canons," 55-57; see also L. Patsavos, "The Canonical Tradition of the Orthodox Church," *A Companion to the Greek Orthodox Church*, ed. by F. Litsas, (New York: Greek Orthodox Archdiocese, 1984), 147.

[15] See Patsavos, "The Canonical," p. 144.

[16] A similar view is expressed by R. Metz in his explanation of the justification for the Church's law/canonical tradition. See *What Is Canon Law?*, 12-14.

[17] See Patsavos, "The Canonical," p. 144.

[18] Translation of this canon is from an unpublished manuscript of canons of the ecumenical synods translated into contemporary English by Prof. John Cavarnos, (no date; hereafter, Cavarnos, "Canons").

[19] Percival, *The Seven*, p. 596.

[20] Percival, p. 432.

[21] See Afanasiev, "The Canons," 57-60.

[22] Kapsanis, *He Poimantike*, 73-82.

[23] Canon 6 of the Second Ecumenical Synod.

[24] Canon 1 of St. Cyril of Alexandria.

[25] Canon 86 of Carthage.

[26] D. Cummings, trans., *The Rudder*, (Chicago: Orthodox Christian Educational Society, 1957), p. li.

[27] My rendering of the translation in Cummings, p. 466.

[28] Cummings, p. 964.

[29] Cummings, p. 673.

[30] Cummings, p. 973.

[31] Kapsanis, *He Poimantike*, 83-90; see also Patsavos, "Ecclesiastical Reform," 3-7.

[32] Cf. Afanasiev, "The Canons," p. 55. The basic question concerning the unchangeable and unrenewable dimension of the canons is treated extensively in the publication by C. Mouratides, *To aionion kyros ton ieron kanonon*, (Athens, 1972). See also P. Boumis, *To kyros kai e ischys ton ieron kanonon*, (Athens, 1975).

[33] See Patsavos, "The Canonical," 142-4.

[34] My rendering of the translation in Cummings, p. li.

[35] Cf. Meyendorff, "Contemporary Problems," 99-100.

[36] See Patsavos, "Ecclesiastical Reform," p. 5.

[37] Patsavos, p. 7.

[38] Kapsanis, *He Poimantike*, 93-112.

[39] Kapsanis, p. 112.

[40] Kapsanis, 113-29. See also my contribution to *The Theological Agenda for the Future of the Greek Orthodox Archdiocese*, Report to His Eminence Archbishop Iakovos (Brookline, MA: Holy Cross Orthodox Press, 1990), entitled "Leadership Issues" (Part Three), 14-18; see as well my article "The Relationship between the Clergy and the People from a Canonical Perspective," taken from the paper used to generate discussion on the immediately preceding topic, published in the periodical *Orthodoxia* 2 (3), 1994.

[41] Kapsanis, *He Poimantike*, 114-5.

[42] Percival, *The Seven*, p. 475.

[43] Book II, Chapter 28.

[44] Kapsanis, *He Poimantike*, 126-9.

[45] Kapsanis, 131-53.

[46] Cavarnos, "Canons."

[47] Canon 1 of St. Peter of Alexandria.

[48] Canons 2 and 3 of St. Peter of Alexandria.

[49] Canon 11 of St. Peter of Alexandria.

[50] Canons 1 and 2 of Sardica.

[51] Canon 26 of the Sixth Ecumenical Synod; canons 27 and 46 of St. Basil.

[52] Canon 8 of St. Peter of Alexandria.

[53] Canon 9 of St. Peter of Alexandria.

[54] Canon 22 of the Seventh Ecumenical Synod.

[55] Cavarnos, "Canons."

[56] Canon 85 of St. Basil.

[57] Canon 31 of the Holy Apostles.

[58] Canon 102 of the Sixth Ecumenical Synod.

[59] Canon 52 of the Holy Apostles.

[60] Canon 11 of St. Peter of Alexandria.

[61] Canon 6 of St. Gregory of Nyssa.

[62] Canon 27 of the Holy Apostles.

[63] Canon 16 of Ancyra.

[64] Canon 16 of Ancyra.

[65] Canon 18 of St. Basil.

[66] Canon 18 of St. Basil.

[67] Canon 46 of the Sixth Ecumenical Synod.

[68] Regarding the principle of "individualization" ("exatomikefsis"), see C. Mouratides, *Christokentrike poimantike en tois "Asketikois" tou Megalou Vasileiou,* (Athens, 1962), 68-70.

[69] Cavarnos, "Canons."

[70] Kapsanis, *He Poimantike,* 155-65.

[71] Canon 6 of the Second Ecumenical Synod.

[72] Percival, *The Seven,* p. 447.

[73] Percival, p. 110.

[74] Kapsanis, *He Poimantike,* 167-84.

[75] Canon 78 of the Sixth Ecumenical Synod.

[76] Canons 22 and 30 of St. Basil.

[77] Canon 22 of St. Basil.

[78] P. L'Huillier, "To diazygion kata tin theologian kai to kanonikon dikaion tis orthodoxou Ekklesias," *Gregorios o Palamas* 621 (1971), 24.

[79] L'Huillier, p. 21.

[80] Canon 4 of St. Basil.

[81] Canon 66 of the Holy Apostles.

[82] Canon 19 of Gangra.

[83] Canon 51 of the Holy Apostles.

[84] This is in harmony with the recommended, but as yet non-binding, decision of the Third Pan-Orthodox Pre-synodal Conference held in 1986 regarding the practice of fasting in the contemporary Church.

[85] See prologues of C. Mouratides and G. Kapsanis in Kapsanis, He poimantike, 11-16, from which much of the assessment which follows is adapted; see also Patsavos, "Ecclesiastical Reform," 7-10.

[86] The christocentric focus of pastoral ministry as understood in the early Church is the basis of the excellent study by C. Mouratides, Christokentrike poimantike.

[87] Scriptural texts are from the Revised Standard Version of the Bible.

[88] See Patsavos, "The Canonical," 142-3.

[89] Regarding the pastoral significance of the canons, see Patsavos, p. 144.

[90] See also my article "Ecclesiastical Reform".

[91] Kapsanis, He Poimantike, 19-33.

[92] Cavarnos, "Canons."

[93] Cavarnos, "Canons."

APPENDIX

CLASSIFICATION OF CANONICAL TRADITION

Introduction

The second part of this publication, which is a subject listing of the holy canons, gives one an overview of the content of our canonical corpus. It is, in fact, the response to a commonly heard complaint, not unfounded, that the canons are inaccessible. What is meant by this observation is that the material contained in the canons is often unknown or overlooked due to lack of organization. This fact has led some to believe that the way to put order into the material of the holy canons is through codification. The absence of a codification of the canonical tradition reflected in the holy canons makes a resource such as this all the more necessary.

The question of codification arouses two kinds of reactions. On the one hand, there are those who do not in principle object to codification but consider it difficult because of the different legal systems in the various Orthodox autocephalous churches. This, they feel, will necessitate a separate codification for each of them. On the other hand, there are others who reject codification entirely as conflicting with the spiritual essence of Orthodoxy. They believe that the deep unity which exists among all the Orthodox Churches in faith and sacramental life can continue to be preserved according to the local traditions of each autocephalous church.

Regardless of whether codification is ever undertaken, a classification of the content of the holy canons has long been needed. A purpose of the present work is to meet this need. It differs from a word index in that it classifies canons under subject headings and is therefore broader in scope. It does not claim to be an exhaustive study of all the canons but rather the beginning of a process of ongoing refinement.

Credit for the original concept of this project belongs to the late Protopresbyter Evangelos Mantzouneas of the Church of Greece. Under the titles *Kanonikos dioiketikos kodiks* (Athens, 1974), *Kanonikos poinikos-epitimiakos kodiks* (Athens, 1973), *Kanonikos dikonomikos kodiks* (Athens, 1974) and *Kanonikos monachikos kodiks* (Athens, 1976), the compiler has divided the material of the holy canons into four codes corresponding to the following categories: administration, penitential discipline, court procedure, and monasticism. These same divisions are retained in the present work with some minor variations.

Given the significance of the concept of systematization and classification of the canons, a set of codes in English corresponding to those in Greek was originally envisioned. However, due to the shortcomings of the volumes in Greek, that plan was abandoned and replaced with the current consolidated version. Although one must applaud any effort to systematize the content of the canons, the fact cannot be overlooked that, as mentioned, there were many errors in the original volumes published in Greek. Consequently, great care has been given in the present work to the correct citation of texts, as well as to the rearrangement of subject headings and canons where necessary.

Owing to the absence of a much-needed modern

translation of the entire collection of canons, the actual text of the canons is omitted and replaced only by the citing of its source (i.e., council or father) and number. Hopefully by the time a future edition of this work appears, it will be accompanied by just such a modern translation. Also omitted are the scriptural texts which precede the canons under many of the subject headings in the original volumes.

Canons are classified on the basis of their content applicability in whole or in part. Classifications and canon selections conform for the most part to those appearing in the original four canonical codes of Protopresbyter Evangelos Mantzouneas in Greek. The order of subject headings and selection of canons are based solely on the preference of that compiler. Such a methodology was pursued solely in the interest of time and for the sake of convenience.

Subject headings are as inclusive as possible. The subject headings listed include the most important canons related to a particular subject. A number of canons listed under certain subject headings may be only remotely related. In such cases, however, one should always look for some common point of reference between them, even if indirect. In other cases, the researcher who studies the unabridged text of a canon cited together with its accompanying commentary and notes will easily recognize its relationship.

The process of refinement necessary in the classification of the canons is arduous indeed. It requires the involvement of many specialists, as the revision of the Code of Canon Law of the Roman Catholic Church in 1983 has shown. Perhaps future stages of growth in the process of refinement will include such involvement. Undoubtedly, the result of a similar undertaking will be a more detailed classification with many more subdivisions. For the time being, however, and as a first step, it is hoped that the present scope of the work provides the incentive for further investigation into the rich content of the canons.

It is furthermore hoped that a future edition of this work will include subject headings for all the canons in our canonical corpus. To this end, the suggestions and recommendations of all those who find this project worthwhile is eagerly sought.

In the original stages of the project, students from my classes of Canon Law taught at Holy Cross School of Theology assisted in the endeavor. Student assignments consisted mainly in the verification of texts and had as their purpose the familiarization with sources as well as with the actual content of the canons themselves. Special mention must be made of my former assistant, Rev. Frank A. Milanese, whose computer skills and overall devotion to the project of classification were of inestimable worth. A debt of lasting gratitude is hereby acknowledged.

I. Canons Related to Administration

1. Presuppositions of Entry into the Clergy and Related Matters

Canonical Age

Sixth Ecumenical Synod, 14, 15

Neocaesarea, 11

Soundness of Mind

Holy Apostles, 79

Soundness of Body

First Ecumenical Synod, 1

Holy Apostles, 21, 22, 77

Examination of Clerical Candidates

Carthage (419), 50

St. Theophilos, 7

St. Cyril, 4

Marriage of the Clergy

Marriage of Minor Clerics

Fourth Ecumenical Synod, 14

Sixth Ecumenical Synod, 6

Holy Apostles, 26

Carthage (419), 16

Marriage of Presbyters

> Sixth Ecumenical Synod, 13

> Holy Apostles, 5

> Gangra, 4

Successive Marriage

> Sixth Ecumenical Synod, 3

> Holy Apostles, 17

> St. Basil, 12

Celibacy of Bishops

> Sixth Ecumenical Synod, 12, 48

Election of Presbyters

> Seventh Ecumenical Synod, 3

> Laodicea, 13

Election of Bishops

> First Ecumenical Synod, 4

> Seventh Ecumenical Synod, 3

> Holy Apostles, 80

> Laodicea, 12

Ordination of Presbyters

> Holy Apostles, 2

> St. Theophilos, 7

Ordination of Bishops

> Holy Apostles, 1

> Antioch, 19

Laodicea, 5

Carthage (419), 13, 49

At Large Ordinations

Fourth Ecumenical Synod, 6

Effective Ordinations

First Ecumenical Synod, 19

Fourth Ecumenical Synod, 2

Sixth Ecumenical Synod, 22

Seventh Ecumenical Synod, 5

Holy Apostles, 29

Ancyra, 13

Antioch, 13, 22

St. Cyril, 4

St. Gennadios, 1

St. Tarasios, Canonical Epistle

Extraterritorial Ordinations

Holy Apostles, 35

Antioch, 13, 22

Reordinations

Holy Apostles, 68

Carthage (419), 27, 48

2. ACTIONS RELATED TO THE MINISTRY OF THE CLERGY

Appointment of Bishops and Other Clerics

Ancyra, 13, 18

Antioch, 17

Sardica, 6, 15, 19

Carthage (419), 98

Exercise of Priestly Authority under Exceptional Circumstances

Sixth Ecumenical Synod, 37

Negligence in the Exercise of Priestly Authority

Holy Apostles, 36

Carthage (419), 121

Transfer/Passage of Bishops and Other Clerics

First Ecumenical Synod, 15, 16

Fourth Ecumenical Synod, 10, 20

Sixth Ecumenical Synod, 17, 18

Seventh Ecumenical Synod, 15

Holy Apostles, 14, 15

Antioch, 3, 21

Sardica, 1, 2, 16, 17

Carthage (419), 71

Resignation of Bishops and Other Clerics

1st-2nd Synod, 16

St. Cyril, 3

Demotion of Bishops

> First Ecumenical Synod, 8
>
> Fourth Ecumenical Synod, 29
>
> Sixth Ecumenical Synod, 20
>
> St. Cyril, 1

3. CANONICAL ORDER

Privileges of the Primate

> First Ecumenical Synod, 6
>
> Fourth Ecumenical Synod, 28
>
> Sixth Ecumenical Synod 36, 39
>
> Holy Apostles, 34
>
> Antioch, 9
>
> Carthage (419), 85

Privileges of Clerics in General

> First Ecumenical Synod, 18
>
> Sixth Ecumenical Synod, 7
>
> Laodicea, 20

Canonical Letters

> Fourth Ecumenical Synod, 13
>
> Holy Apostles, 33
>
> Antioch, 7, 11, 13
>
> Laodicea, 42
>
> Carthage (419), 77, 85, 106

Breach of Responsibility

Fourth Ecumenical Synod, 20, 25

Sixth Ecumenical Synod, 80

Holy Apostles, 36, 39, 58

1st-2nd Synod, 3

Antioch, 17

4. CANONICAL ORDERLINESS

Clerics of a Foreign Diocese

First Ecumenical Synod, 16

Fourth Ecumenical Synod, 5, 13, 20

Sixth Ecumenical Synod, 17, 18, 20

Holy Apostles, 12, 33

Antioch, 7, 8

Sardica, 15

Unauthorized Entry into a Foreign Diocese or Parish

Neocaesarea, 13

Antioch, 13, 22

Sardica, 3

Carthage (419), 56

Passage of Clerics from City to City

First Ecumenical Synod, 15

Sardica, 2, 12, 20

Representation of Bishops

5. ADMINISTRATION

Synods

First Ecumenical Synod, 5

Second Ecumenical Synod, 6

Fourth Ecumenical Synod, 19

Sixth Ecumenical Synod, 8

Seventh Ecumenical Synod, 6

Holy Apostles, 37

Antioch, 16, 18, 20

Laodicea, 40

Carthage (419), 18, 51, 76, 77

Administrative Functionaries

Metropolitans

First Ecumenical Synod, 6

Fourth Ecumenical Synod, 9, 17, 25

Seventh Ecumenical Synod, 11

1st-2nd Synod, 14, 15

Antioch, 9, 11

Bishops

First Ecumenical Synod, 8

Fourth Ecumenical Synod, 2, 16, 29

Seventh Ecumenical Synod, 3, 4

Holy Apostles, 29, 30, 32, 34, 76

1st-2nd Synod, 16

Antioch, 9, 10, 11, 12, 13, 14, 15, 18, 23, 25

Laodicea, 12, 13, 57

Sardica, 3, 7, 8, 11, 12

Carthage (419), 67

St. Cyril, 1

"Chorepiscopi" (Auxiliary Bishops)

First Ecumenical Synod, 8

Ancyra, 13

Neocaesarea, 14

Antioch, 10

St. Basil, 89

6. Clerics

Presbyters

First Ecumenical Synod, 15, 16, 18

Sixth Ecumenical Synod, 14

Holy Apostles, 2, 5, 8, 36, 39, 45, 52, 53, 56, 59, 63

1st-2nd Synod, 11

Ancyra, 1, 14

Neocaesarea, 1, 7, 8, 9, 11, 12, 13

Antioch, 3

Laodicea, 20, 24, 56, 57, 58

Carthage (419), 6, 7, 9, 10, 11, 12, 20, 25, 27, 28, 33

Deacons

First Ecumenical Synod, 18

Sixth Ecumenical Synod, 13, 14, 16

Holy Apostles, 2, 25, 27, 28, 29, 32, 33, 36

Ancyra, 2, 10

Laodicea, 20

Deaconesses

First Ecumenical Synod, 19

Fourth Ecumenical Synod, 15

Sixth Ecumenical Synod, 14, 40

St. Basil, 44

Minor Clerics

Holy Apostles, 26

Laodicea, 15, 21, 22, 23

Carthage (419), 90

7. ADMINISTRATIVE OPERATION

Obligatory Attendance at Meetings of the Synod

Fourth Ecumenical Synod, 19

Sixth Ecumenical Synod, 8

Seventh Ecumenical Synod, 6

Laodicea, 40

Carthage (419), 76

Obedience to the Superior

Fourth Ecumenical Synod, 13

Holy Apostles, 31, 39

1st-2nd Synod, 14

Sardica, 1, 2, 3

Carthage (419), 31, 122

Dereliction of Duty

Sixth Ecumenical Synod, 18

Antioch, 17

Sardica, 18

Neglect of a Diocese/Parish

1st-2nd Synod, 16

Antioch, 3

Carthage (419), 71, 121

Division of a Metropolis

Fourth Ecumenical Synod, 12

Presuppositions for Establishing Autocephalous Churches

Fourth Ecumenical Synod, 17

Sixth Ecumenical Synod, 38

8. AUTHORITY OF BISHOPS OVER MONASTERIES AND INSTITUTIONS

Establishment of Monasteries

9. HOLY MYSTERIES

Holy Apostles, 1, 2, 17, 18, 19, 21, 22, 29, 61, 68, 77, 78, 79

1st-2nd Synod, 17

Laodicea, 3, 5

Sardica, 10, 15

Carthage (419), 27, 36, 48, 49, 50

St. Basil, 12

St. Theophilos, 7, 12

St. Tarasios, 1

Marriage

Marriage in General

Holy Apostles, 26

Gangra, 1, 4, 10, 14

Laodicea, 53, 54

St. Basil, 26

Sanctity of Marriage

Laodicea, 53, 54

St. Basil, 9

Mixed Marriages

Fourth Ecumenical Synod, 14

Sixth Ecumenical Synod, 72

Laodicea, 10, 31

Carthage (419), 21

Impediments of Marriage

St. Basil, 87

II. Canons Related to Penitential Discipline Invoked in Ecclesiastical Courts

1. Offenses against Orthodox Faith

Heresy

Second Ecumenical Synod, 1, 6

Third Ecumenical Synod, 1, 2, 4, 6, 7

Sixth Ecumenical Synod, 1, 81

Seventh Ecumenical Synod, 1, 9

Holy Apostles, 45, 46, 64

Laodicea, 32, 33, 34, 35

Carthage (419), 109, 111, 112, 113, 114, 115, 116

St. Basil, 1, 5, 20

Apostasy

First Ecumenical Synod, 10, 11, 14

Sixth Ecumenical Synod, 94

Holy Apostles, 62

Ancyra, 1, 2, 3, 4, 5, 6, 7, 8, 9

St. Peter, 1, 2, 3, 4, 5, 6, 7, 8, 9, 10, 11, 12, 13

St. Basil, 73, 81

St. Gregory (Nyssa), 2

2. OFFENSES AGAINST ECCLESIAL STRUCTURE

Schism

Holy Apostles, 31

1st-2nd Synod, 13, 14, 15

Antioch, 5

Carthage (419), 9, 10, 11, 67, 124

St. Basil, 1

Clandestine Meeting

Holy Apostles, 31

Antioch, 5

St. Basil, 1

Conspiracy, Factionalism, Machination

Fourth Ecumenical Synod, 18

Sixth Ecumenical Synod, 34

Simony

Sixth Ecumenical Synod, 22, 23

Seventh Ecumenical Synod, 3, 4, 5, 19

Holy Apostles, 29

St. Basil, 90

3. OFFENSES CONTRARY TO CANONICAL ORDER

Breach of Responsibility

Second Ecumenical Synod, 2

Fourth Ecumenical Synod, 10, 20, 25

Contempt of Ecclesiastical Authority

Renunciation of Monastic Vows

Renunciation of Priesthood

Carthage (419), 60, 61

Improper Dress of Clerics

Sixth Ecumenical Synod, 27, 42

Seventh Ecumenical Synod, 16

Physical Abuse

Holy Apostles, 27

1st-2nd Synod, 9

4. Offenses against God

Denial of God

First Ecumenical Synod, 10

Holy Apostles, 62

Ancyra, 1, 2

St. Basil, 73

Violation of Oath

St. Basil, 10, 17, 29, 64, 82

Perjury

Holy Apostles, 25

St. John (Faster), 31

Soothsaying, Magic, Sorcery

Sixth Ecumenical Synod, 61, 65

Ancyra, 24

Laodicea, 36

St. Basil, 7, 65, 72, 83

Sixth Ecumenical Synod, 91

St. Basil, 8

St. John (Faster), 21

Infant Exposure (Moral Complicity)

St. John (Faster), 26

6. Offenses against Marriage

Adultery

Holy Apostles, 61

Ancyra, 20

Neocaesarea, 1, 8

St. Basil, 60

St. Theophilos, 3

Second Marriage

Sixth Ecumenical Synod, 3

Laodicea, 1

St. Basil, 4, 12

St. Nicephoros, 2

Abhorrence of Marriage

Sixth Ecumenical Synod, 13

Holy Apostles, 5, 51

Gangra, 14

Adultery Committed by the Spouse of a Presbyter

Neocaesarea, 8

7. OFFENSES CONTRARY TO MORAL ORDER

Fornication (with an Unspecified Person)

Sixth Ecumenical Synod, 44

Holy Apostles, 25

Neocaesarea, 1

St. Basil, 3, 18, 19, 44, 59, 60, 70, 88

St. Gregory (Nyssa), 4

St. Nicephoros, 35, 36

Panderism

Sixth Ecumenical Synod, 86

Promiscuity with an Adult or Adolescent Male

St. Basil, 7, 62

Abduction

Fourth Ecumenical Synod, 27

Sixth Ecumenical Synod, 92

Bestiality

Ancyra, 17

St. Basil, 7, 63

St. Nicephoros, 28

Mutual Act of Impurity

St. John (Faster), 9

Emissions

St. Dionysios, 4

St. Athanasios, 1

St. Timothy, 12

St. John (Faster), 6, 7

Inappropriate Physical Contact with a Woman

St. Basil, 70

St. John (Faster), 11

Cohabitation

First Ecumenical Synod, 3

Sixth Ecumenical Synod, 5

Ancyra, 19

St. Basil, 88

Frequenting Public Baths

Sixth Ecumenical Synod, 77

Laodicea, 30

Boisterous Behavior at Public Feasts

Ancyra, 7

Neocaesarea, 7

Laodicea, 24, 55

Contact between Men/Women in Monasteries

Sixth Ecumenical Synod, 47

Seventh Ecumenical Synod, 20

8. Offenses against Property

Greed

Carthage (419), 5

9. OFFENSES AGAINST PERSONS

Insulting a Bishop

Holy Apostles, 55

Insulting Presbyters and Deacons

Holy Apostles, 56

Insulting Persons of Authority

Holy Apostles, 84

Lack of Respect for the Disabled

Holy Apostles, 57

Failure to Share with Those in Need

Holy Apostles, 4, 41, 59

10. CANONICAL PROHIBITIONS

Sunday Rest and Canonical Feasts

Laodicea, 29

Respect for the House of God and Holy Utensils

Sixth Ecumenical Synod, 88, 97

Holy Apostles, 73

1st-2nd Synod, 10

The Use, Reading and Safe-keeping of Canonical Books

Sixth Ecumenical Synod, 68

Seventh Ecumenical Synod, 9

Holy Apostles, 60

Canonical Observance of Pascha

Holy Apostles, 7, 70

Antioch, 1

Fasting on Saturday, Sunday and during the Great Fast

Sixth Ecumenical Synod, 55, 89

Holy Apostles, 66

Gangra, 18

Laodicea, 50

St. Timothy, 10

11. Offenses Contrary to Administrative Operation

Extraterritorial Ordinations

Holy Apostles, 35

Antioch, 13, 22

Participation of Bishops in Synods

Fourth Ecumenical Synod, 19

Sixth Ecumenical Synod, 8

Seventh Ecumenical Synod, 6

Carthage (419), 76, 95

Execution of Administrative Decisions

Fourth Ecumenical Synod, 26

1st-2nd Synod, 13, 14

Carthage (419), 31, 67, 121, 122, 123

Division of a Metropolis

Fourth Ecumenical Synod, 12

Accepting Clerics of a Foreign Diocese

Fourth Ecumenical Synod, 13, 20

Sixth Ecumenical Synod, 17

Laodicea, 42

Carthage (419), 9, 29

Dereliction of Duty

Antioch, 17

Sardica, 19

Neglect of a Diocese/Parish

Antioch, 3, 17

Sardica, 19

Conflicting Responsibilities

Fourth Ecumenical Synod, 3, 7

Seventh Ecumenical Synod, 11

1st-2nd Synod, 11

Extraterritorial Divine Services

Seventh Ecumenical Synod, 10

Abandonment of a Monastery

Seventh Ecumenical Synod, 21

1st-2nd Synod, 4

Election of an Abbot from a Foreign Monastery

Carthage (419), 80

III. Canons Related to Penitential Discipline Invoked by Spiritual Fathers during Holy Confession

1. Offenses against Orthodox Faith

Heresy

> Third Ecumenical Synod, 6
>
> Fourth Ecumenical Synod, 14
>
> Sixth Ecumenical Synod, 1
>
> Holy Apostles, 45, 46, 71
>
> Gangra, 20
>
> Laodicea, 9, 32, 33, 34
>
> Carthage (419), 110, 111, 112, 113, 114
>
> St. Peter, 14
>
> St. Timothy, 9
>
> St. Nicephoros, 17

Apostasy

> First Ecumenical Synod, 11, 12
>
> Third Ecumenical Synod, 7
>
> Holy Apostles, 70
>
> Ancyra, 7, 8, 9
>
> Laodicea, 35
>
> St. Gregory (Neocaesarea), 7

St. Peter, 1, 10, 11

St. Basil, 73, 81

Observance of non-Christian Feasts

Holy Apostles, 70

Laodicea, 29, 37, 38, 39

2. OFFENSES AGAINST GOD

Blasphemy

Holy Apostles, 62

Ancyra, 1, 2

Gangra, 5

St. Basil, 73

St. John (Faster), 4

Violation of Oath

St. Basil, 10, 29

Perjury

St. Basil, 64, 82

St. John (Faster), 31

Soothsaying, Magic, Sorcery

Sixth Ecumenical Synod, 61, 62, 65

Ancyra, 24

Laodicea, 36

St. Basil, 72

St. Gregory (Nyssa), 3

4. OFFENSES AGAINST HUMAN LIFE

Physical Violence

Voluntary Murder

Involuntary Murder

Murder in War

Infant Exposure

Abortion

St. Basil, 2

St. John (Faster), 21

Suicide

St. Timothy, 14

Self-mutilation

Holy Apostles, 22, 24

Castration

1st-2nd Synod, 8

Lack of Respect for the Disabled

Holy Apostles, 57

5. OFFENSES AGAINST MARRIAGE

Adultery (with an Unspecified Person)

Sixth Ecumenical Synod, 98

Holy Apostles, 48

Ancyra, 20

St. Basil, 39, 58

St. John (Faster), 13

Adultery (with a Specified Person)

Ancyra, 25

St. Basil, 75, 76, 78, 79

St. John (Faster), 15, 16

Incest

St. John (Faster), 14

Second Marriage

Sixth Ecumenical Synod, 3

Laodicea, 1

St. Basil, 4, 12

St. Nicephoros, 2

Third Marriage

Neocaesarea, 3

St. Basil, 4, 80

St. Nicephoros, 2

Abhorrence of Marriage

Gangra, 1, 4, 9, 10, 14

Abandonment of a Spouse

Gangra, 14

St. Basil, 35, 46, 48, 77

Illicit Marriage

Sixth Ecumenical Synod, 53, 54, 72, 93

Neocaesarea, 2, 3

St. Basil, 9, 68

Abandonment of Children by Parents

Gangra, 15

Lack of Filial Respect towards Parents

Gangra, 16

St. Basil, 38

6. OFFENSES CONTRARY TO MORAL ORDER

Fornication (with an Unspecified Person)

Sixth Ecumenical Synod, 44

Holy Apostles, 25

Ancyra, 19

St. Basil, 6, 19, 25, 59

St. John (Faster), 12

St. Nicephoros, 33, 35, 36

Fornication (with a Specified Person)

St. Basil, 67, 75

St. John (Faster), 14, 15, 16

Panderism

Sixth Ecumenical Synod, 86

Promiscuity

St. Basil, 7

St. John (Faster), 18

Bestiality

Ancyra, 16

St. Basil, 7

St. Nicephoros, 28

Pederasty

St. John (Faster), 19

Self-abuse

St. John (Faster), 10

Mutual Act of Impurity

> St. John (Faster), 9

Emissions

> St. Athanasios, 1

> St. John (Faster), 6, 7

Abduction

> Sixth Ecumenical Synod, 92

> St. Basil, 30

Cross-dressing as the Opposite Sex

> Gangra, 13

7. OFFENSES AGAINST PROPERTY

Greed

> St. Gregory (Neocaesarea), 2, 3, 4, 5, 9

Robbery

> St. Gregory (Nyssa), 6

Theft

> Holy Apostles, 25

> St. Basil, 61

> St. John (Faster), 27, 28

Violation of Graves

> St. Basil, 66

> St. Gregory (Nyssa), 7

> St. John (Faster), 29

Sacrilege

Holy Apostles, 72, 73

1st-2nd Synod, 10

St. Gregory (Nyssa), 8

Speculation, Lending at Interest

St. Basil, 14

St. Nicephoros, 31

Gambling

Sixth Ecumenical Synod, 50

Holy Apostles, 42, 43

8. OFFENSES AGAINST PERSONS

Insulting Persons of Authority

Holy Apostles, 84

Contempt of Ecclesiastical Authority

Sixth Ecumenical Synod, 64

Offense of Family Honor

Sixth Ecumenical Synod, 87, 92, 93, 98

St. Basil, 21, 25, 31

9. VARIOUS PROHIBITIONS

Intoxication

Holy Apostles, 42, 43

Concerning Menstruation

    St. Dionysios, 2

    St. Timothy, 7

    St. John (Faster), 17

Physical Contact of Men/Women

    St. John (Faster), 11

Marital Relations of Spouses

    St. Timothy, 13

Death of an Unbaptized Infant

    St. John (Faster), 24

Molestation of a Child

    St. John (Faster), 19

Involuntary Murder of an Infant

    St. John (Faster), 23

Consumption of Spoiled Food

    St. John (Faster), 34

Ejection of Holy Communion

    St. John (Faster), 35

Offerings of Persons Guilty of Impurity

    St. Nicephoros, 33

IV. Canons Related to Ecclesiastical Court Procedure

1. Presuppositions of Ecclesiastical Penitential Courts

Ecclesiastical Penitential Courts in General

Composition of a Canonical Offense

Accusers of Clerics

Law of Retaliation Inflicted upon Accusers

Competencies of Ecclesiastical Penitential Courts

Competency as to Jurisdiction

Competency as to Place

First Ecumenical Synod, 15

Second Ecumenical Synod, 6

Fourth Ecumenical Synod, 9, 10, 20

Composition of Ecclesiastical Penitential Courts

Second Ecumenical Synod, 6

Carthage (419), 12, 14, 20, 107

Charges against Clerics

Second Ecumenical Synod, 6

Fourth Ecumenical Synod, 9

Holy Apostles, 74

Witnesses against Clerics

Suitability of Witnesses

Second Ecumenical Synod, 6

Holy Apostles, 75

Carthage (419), 59, 128, 129, 131

St. Theophilos, 9

Juvenile Witnesses

Carthage (419), 131

2. PRELIMINARY PROCEDURE

Penal Charge

St. Gregory (Nyssa), 4

Penal Inquiry

Holy Apostles, 74

Evidence

First Ecumenical Synod, 2

Second Ecumenical Synod, 6

Holy Apostles, 61

Neocaesarea, 9

Summons and Defense of a Defendant

Holy Apostles, 74

Carthage (419), 12, 15, 19, 20, 87

St. Cyril, 1

Confession of a Defendant

Holy Apostles, 74

Neocaesarea, 9

St. Gregory (Nyssa), 4

3. CONCERNING COURTS

Episcopal Courts

Holy Apostles, 32

Antioch, 4, 5, 6, 11, 12, 14, 15

Sardica, 14

Carthage (419), 10, 11, 19, 20, 107

Synodal Courts

Second Ecumenical Synod, 6

Appeal to a Superior Ecclesiastical Authority

Fourth Ecumenical Synod, 17

Sardica, 3, 4, 14

Pardon

First Ecumenical Synod, 5, 8, 12, 13

Holy Apostles, 32, 52

Ancyra, 1, 2, 6, 7

Antioch, 4, 6

Laodicea, 2

St. Basil, 1

St. Gregory (Nyssa), 4, 5, 7

Competent Authority for Granting Pardon

First Ecumenical Synod, 12, 13

Holy Apostles, 32

Ancyra, 5

5. POST-TRIAL CONSEQUENCES

Universal Validity of Ecclesiastical Penalties

Holy Apostles, 10, 11, 12, 16, 32, 33

Sardica, 13

Carthage (419), 9, 62, 133

Disobedience to the Decisions of Ecclesiastical Courts

Fourth Ecumenical Synod, 20

Holy Apostles, 11, 12, 16

Antioch, 4

Sardica, 13

Carthage (419), 9, 10, 29, 62

V. CANONS RELATED TO MONASTICISM

1. PRESUPPOSITIONS OF THE MONASTIC STATE

Free Consent

Sixth Ecumenical Synod, 40, 43

St. Basil, 18

Canonical Age

Sixth Ecumenical Synod, 40

Carthage (419), 126

St. Basil, 18

Novitiate

Sixth Ecumenical Synod, 41

Seventh Ecumenical Synod, 19

1st-2nd Synod, 5

2. CANONICITY OF THE MONASTIC STATE

Acquisition of the Monastic State

Fourth Ecumenical Synod, 4, 8, 24

Sixth Ecumenical Synod, 40, 42, 43, 49

Seventh Ecumenical Synod, 13, 20

1st-2nd Synod, 2

Holy Wisdom, 2

Place of Acquisition of the Monastic State

Sixth Ecumenical Synod, 41, 42

1st-2nd Synod, 2

Simoniacs

Fourth Ecumenical Synod, 2

Seventh Ecumenical Synod, 19

3. VALIDITY OF THE MONASTIC STATE

Tonsure of Monks

Sixth Ecumenical Synod, 42, 43

1st-2nd Synod, 2, 5, 6

St. Nicephoros, 6

Tonsure of Nuns

Sixth Ecumenical Synod, 45

1st-2nd Synod, 6

Carthage (419), 6, 44

Repetition of Laying on of Hands

St. Nicephoros, 14

4. MONASTIC PROFESSION

Chastity

Fourth Ecumenical Synod, 15, 16

Sixth Ecumenical Synod, 44

Ancyra, 19

Exit of Monks from the Monastery

Fourth Ecumenical Synod, 4, 23

Sixth Ecumenical Synod, 41, 46

Seventh Ecumenical Synod, 21

1st-2nd Synod, 3, 4

Carthage (419), 80

St. Nicephoros, 17, 24

Exit of Nuns from the Monastery

Sixth Ecumenical Synod, 46

Seventh Ecumenical Synod, 21

1st-2nd Synod, 3, 4

Change of Monastery

Fourth Ecumenical Synod, 4

Sixth Ecumenical Synod, 46

Seventh Ecumenical Synod, 21

1st-2nd Synod, 3, 4

Carthage (419), 80

St. Nicephoros, 17

6. INTERNAL ORDERLINESS IN MONASTERIES

Monks

Abbot

Sixth Ecumenical Synod, 41, 46

Seventh Ecumenical Synod, 19

1st-2nd Synod, 2, 3

Relations of Nuns and Monks

Seventh Ecumenical Synod, 20

Confinement within the Monastery

Sixth Ecumenical Synod, 46

Divorce and Tonsure of the Wife of an Episcopal Candidate

Sixth Ecumenical Synod, 48

7. MONKS IN COMMON LAW

In General

Fourth Ecumenical Synod, 3, 7

Sixth Ecumenical Synod, 24, 34

Law of Inheritance

1st-2nd Synod, 6

Family Law

Fourth Ecumenical Synod, 3

St. Basil, 6

General Principles of Law

Fourth Ecumenical Synod, 3

Administrative Law

Fourth Ecumenical Synod, 7

Commercial Law

Seventh Ecumenical Synod, 13

Civil Procedural Law

Fourth Ecumenical Synod, 3

8. CONCERNING MONASTERIES

In General

Fourth Ecumenical Synod, 4, 8, 24

Sixth Ecumenical Synod, 41, 42, 43, 45, 46, 49

Seventh Ecumenical Synod, 12, 13, 14, 17, 18, 19, 20

1st-2nd Synod, 1, 2, 3, 4, 5, 6

Privately Owned Monasteries

1st-2nd Synod, 7

Canonical Monasteries

Fourth Ecumenical Synod, 4, 8, 24

Sixth Ecumenical Synod, 49

Seventh Ecumenical Synod, 12, 13, 17, 20

1st-2nd Synod, 1

Sanctity of Monasteries

Sixth Ecumenical Synod, 49

Seventh Ecumenical Synod, 13

1st-2nd Synod, 4

Prohibition of Trespass

Sixth Ecumenical Synod, 47, 48

Seventh Ecumenical Synod, 18

Established Order of Monasteries

Sixth Ecumenical Synod, 45, 46

Seventh Ecumenical Synod, 22

1st-2nd Synod, 6

Administration of Monasteries

Bishop

Fourth Ecumenical Synod, 3, 4, 8

1st-2nd Synod, 1, 3, 4

Abbot

Sixth Ecumenical Synod, 41, 46

Seventh Ecumenical Synod, 21

1st-2nd Synod, 2, 3

Management of Monasteries

Seventh Ecumenical Synod, 11, 12, 13

Holy Apostles, 38, 41

1st-2nd Synod, 1, 6, 7

9. Monastic Systems

Coenobitic System

Fourth Ecumenical Synod, 4

Sixth Ecumenical Synod, 46

Seventh Ecumenical Synod, 22

St. Nicephoros, 19

Idiorrhythmic System

Sixth Ecumenical Synod, 42

1st-2nd Synod, 6

10. Monastic Property

Authority over Monastic Property

Personal Property of Monks and Nuns

Appropriation of Monastic Property

Inalienability of Monastic Property